COLOUR CLOSE-UP

WORLD WAR II
WEHRMACHT VEHICLES

COLOUR CLOSE-UP

WORLD WAR II
WEHRMACHT VEHICLES

Jan Suermondt

The Crowood Press

First published in 2003 by
The Crowood Press Ltd
Ramsbury, Marlborough
Wiltshire SN8 2HR

www.crowood.com

© Jan Suermondt 2003

British Library Cataloguing-in-Publication Data
A catalogue record for this book is available from
the British Library

ISBN 1 86126 426 7

Edited by Martin Windrow
Designed by Frank Ainscough/Compendium
Colour Origination by Black Cat Graphics Ltd. Bristol
Printed and bound in Singapore by Craft Print International

Author's note
A book of this size obviously does not offer anything approaching a com-
prehensive guide to Wehrmacht vehicles of World War II; rather, together
with the companion volume on Allied vehicles, it aims to provide a detailed
look at a representative cross-section of such vehicles. It is also unusual in
that, through the the use of an analytical approach to photography, a much
more detailed source of visual reference has been created than is the norm.
A decision was made early on to include interiors where possible, and to
provide close-up shots of some of the more interesting details.

The selection of subjects may at first appear somewhat arbitrary, but
was naturally dictated by the availability of preserved examples suitable for
photography. I apologise in advance to those readers who feel that there
are glaring omissions; depending upon the reception of this book I shall
endeavour to produce additional volumes to fill some of the gaps.

Many thanks are owed to all those vehicle owners and restorers whose
blood, sweat and tears have gone into preserving these vehicles, and without whom this book would not have been possible.

Jan Suermondt
Torquay, Devon
2003

CONTENTS

BMW R12

Bayerische Motoren Werke AG of Munich (BMW) started to produce the R12 motorcyle, a commercial model impressed into military service, in 1935, and continued to manufacture them until the end of 1941. The R12 was an instant success with the motorcycling public throughout Germany and other European countries, due to the fact that it had a robust, reliable engine and an exceptionally smooth ride due to its oil-filled hydraulic front forks.

The R12 was ideally suited to military service, and the majority of the approximately 36,000 produced saw service during World War II. Over 20,000 were produced as civilian models, but most of these were requisitioned by the military; the remaining 10,000 or so were produced to military specifications. The R12 was in service with the Wehrmacht throughout the war and in every theatre of operations.

There were subtle changes in the specification for military use. These were mainly the use of foot pegs instead of the civilian aluminium foot boards, extra strengthening around the steering yolk, and pressed steel rear foot rests rather than aluminium. The military machine was also provided with leather panniers and masked lighting. The R12 was fitted with a 750cc, 4-stroke, 2-cylinder flat twin engine producing 18bhp. It had a 4-speed gearbox and shaft drive transmission, and weighed 408lbs.

The two examples illustrated are both finished in the standard early-war dark grey of the Wehrmacht: a solo machine, and one fitted with the standard (Einheits) sidecar. This was suitable for mounting an MG34 machine gun, and could also be used to transport a light mortar with a few rounds of amunition. In these photographs the machine gun is covered, and stowed in clamps on the left side of the sidecar. The marking on the sidecar is that of the reconnaissance element of the 1st SS Panzer Corps 'Leibstandarte Adolf Hitler'.

BMW R35

Like the R12 (top left), this motorcycle was originally a commercial type. Powered by a 350cc engine, the R35 was used as a solo machine (below) and as part of a combination. The combination illustrated is fitted with the Einheits sidecar, and again is painted in the overall dark grey factory finish which was standard prior to June 1943. The marking is not particular to a specific division but is the universal tactical sign for a motorcycle unit.

BMW R75

The R75 was a specialised military model developed by BMW for the German army. It was intended primarily as a cross-country, heavy sidecar outfit for personnel and equipment transportation, armed reconnaissance and convoy control, but was also used as a solo machine. The R75 was in production from 1940 to 1944; a total of 16,510 were built, and it was to be seen in every German theatre of operations from its introduction into service until the end of the war in Europe. The machine proved successful in operation, and was copied in the Soviet Union as the M72, which remained in service with the Soviet army until 1956.

When functioning as a motorcycle combination the R75 was generally fitted with the Einheits (standard) sidecar which could mount an MG34 or later MG42 machine gun. The wheel of the side car was driven via a shaft leading from a power take-off on the transmission. The motorcycle itself was fitted with a shaft drive transmission; the gearbox provides four forward speeds and one reverse, plus an additional three speeds in a lower ratio for off-road use. The R75 was fitted with a 746cc engine producing 26bhp and had a maximum speed of 57mph. The total unladen weight of the motorbike and sidecar combination was 925lb. Overall dimensions, including sidecar, are: length, 94.4ins; width, 68.1ins; height, 39.3ins. The examples illustrated here show one machine in the overall Dunkelgelb (dark yellow) factory finish introduced as standard for Wehrmacht vehicles and equipment from June 1943; and one camouflaged at unit level with the additional Dunkelgrün (dark green) and Rotbraun (red brown) paints which were issued for field application over the basic dark yellow.

(Left) The carrying capacity of motorcycle combinations could even be increased by the addition of a two-wheel trailer to the sidecar, here towed by an R75 combination. The modern civilian number plate and reflector triangle should, of course, be ignored.

(Below) BMW R61 solo motorcycle. Manufactured at least until the end of 1939, this was powered by a 600cc, 18bhp side valve engine.

Guzzi Trialce
Portamitraglia Pesante

The Guzzi Trialce was a specialised military motor tricycle developed for the Italian Army from the Alce motorcycle. It was used for general load carrying and as a heavy machine gun carrier. The example shown here has steel-reinforced locating holes in the floor of the cargo body to receive the spiked feet of a machine gun tripod.

The Guzzi Trialce was produced from 1940 to 1943 and was widely used throughout the Italian army's campaigns. Fitted with a 499cc single-cylinder engine producing 31.2bhp, the Trialce had a maximum speed of 50 mph, and its unladen weight was 783lbs. Overall dimensions are: length, 9ft 3ins; width, 4ft 1in; height, 3ft 5ins.

Kettenkraftrad SdKfz 2

The Kliene Kettenkraftrad or 'Kettenkrad' was unique in being a half-track motorcycle. It was originally developed for use as a tractor to tow the light guns of the paratroop and air-landing units. With this in mind the vehicle was designed so that it could be transported in a Junkers Ju52/3m aircraft, the standard transport type of the Luftwaffe.

The Kettenkrad was fitted with motorcycle-type front forks, and its tracks were a scaled-down version of those found on the larger half-tracks. The driver was provided with a motorcycle saddle, and two passengers could be accommodated on a rear-facing bench seat. Entering service in 1941, the Kettenkrad first saw action in the airborne invasion of Crete, where it was employed to transport supplies and ammunition and to tow light artillery pieces. It remained in use with the Luftwaffe's airborne troops until the end of the war; it was also used by the army, seeing action in North Africa, on the

Eastern Front, in NW Europe and Italy. When used as a supply vehicle it often towed a light trailer, and in its artillery tractor role it was used to tow the 28mm and 37mm anti-tank guns and the 75mm light field howitzer. There were two other variants of the basic half-track, the Sdkfz 2/1 and the Sdkfz 2/2, both of them telephone cable layers; the first was equipped to handle lightweight cable and the second, heavy duty cable.

The Kettenkrad was produced by NSU and Stoewer, a total of 8,345 being completed before production ceased in 1944. The Kliene Kettenkraftrad Sdkfz 2 was fitted with an Opel Olympia 38 water-cooled petrol engine which produced 36bhp. Maximum speed was 50mph, and it could tow up to 0.45 of a ton. It carried a crew of three – in considerable comfort, even over very rough ground – and weighed 1.2 tons. Overall dimensions are: length, 9ft; width, 3ft 3ins; and height, 3ft 4ins.

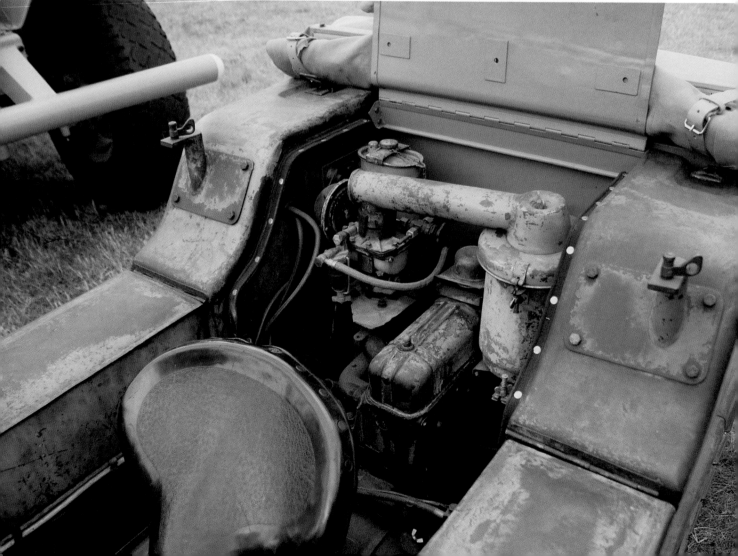

Ver. Klasse III   0.325 t

Auto-Union/Horch Kfz 70 Mannschaftskraftwagen

Throughout the period of Germany's re-armament the limitations of the Treaty of Versailles, and later those imposed by economic considerations, led to the adoption of a profusion of different vehicles that were basically commercially available models adapted to military use. The most common of these, since they were cheap to produce, were personnel carriers based on commercial car chassis, fitted with a simple open body with canvas side screens instead of doors, a canvas hood and bucket seats. This style of body became known as the Kubelsitzer ('bucket-seater') and the cars, unofficially, as Kubelwagens ('bucket cars'). Although these vehicles had a very limited cross-country performance, they were soon found to be useful in service; and when the National Socialist government was voted into power in 1933 they played a significant part in the programme to expand and mechanise the army.

Once Germany's re-armament programme was underway, however, consideration was given to the next generation of vehicles for the armed forces. One of the unfortunate consequences of the decision to use commercially based vehicles was the vast diversity of models taken onto the inventory, with consequent problems of maintenance and the supply of spare parts. The existing field cars had been categorised into three classes of vehicle in 1933:

Leichte Personenkraftwagen ('light passenger car'), of approved models up to 1500cc engine capacity.

Mittlerer Personenkraftwagen ('medium passenger car'), of approved models up to 3000cc engine capacity.

Schwerer Personenkraftwagen ('heavy passenger car'), of approved models over 3000cc engine capacity.

In 1934 a decision was taken to replace the existing commercially based chassis with a new range of standardised chassis types designed specifically for military use as part of a rationalisation scheme known as the Einheits programme (Einheitsfahrgestell – 'standard motor chassis'). There was to be one chassis type for each of the three classes of field car, with as much commonality of components as possible between the three types.

Auto-Union/Horch were selected as producers of both the medium and heavy chassis, and the Auto-Union/Horch Chassis I for heavy passenger cars was produced in 1935. As part of the rationalisation process, it was also intended to use this chassis in a rear-engined form for four-wheeled armoured cars, and this became known as the Sdkfz 221, 222 and 223 series.

Initially all production was taken up by armoured cars, since this was the most pressing need, and manufcture of passenger cars did not begin until 1938.

The front-engined chassis for passenger cars was designated Chassis II, and early vehicles were fitted with four-wheel steering. This soon became viewed as being of dubious benefit, and indeed at speeds in excess of 13mph the rear wheel steering had to be disengaged as it produced dangerous handling characteristics. Consequently, from 1940 onwards rear-wheel steering was no longer fitted. At about this time the Berlin Ford factory also became engaged in production; Ford-built vehicles were externally similar but were fitted with a Ford 3.6 litre V8 78hp engine in place of the Horch unit. A novel feature of early vehicles was the provision of a recess either side of the body in which the spare wheels were free to rotate on stub axles mounted on the chassis. This arrangement prevented the car 'bellying' in rough going, but was discontinued in 1940 in favour of a simpler design with flat body sides to ease produc-

tion. It is one of these latter vehicles that is illustrated here and on page 20. Production ceased in 1941 when, due to further rationalisation under the 1938 Schell-Programm, it was decided that all heavy passenger cars should share the chassis of the 1.5-ton light truck. However, the Auto Union/Horch heavy cars remained in service and were widely used on all fronts until the end of the war.

The heavy passenger car was also used as the basis of several special purpose vehicles, some of which utilised the standard body but with alterations in equipment and stowage, e.g. the Kfz 13 telephone truck, Kfz 83 light searchlight truck, Kfz 59 light gun tractor, and Kfz 81 light anti-aircraft vehicle. Some were fitted with a closed van-type body, such as the Kfz 31 ambulance and the Kfz 24 maintenance truck.

The Auto Union/Horch Kfz 70 was fitted with an Auto Union/Horch 81bhp, 3,823cc V8 engine. It carried a crew of six including the driver, and its dimensions are: length, 15ft 11ins; width, 6ft 6.75ins; height, 6ft 8.25ins.

Stoewer 40 Kfz 1 light field car

The ordnance number given to light passenger cars under the system introduced in 1933, when the Reichswehr was transformed into the Wermacht by the new National Socialist government, was Kfz 1. As already mentioned, at this time a multitude of different models based on commercial vehicles were in simultaneous service, causing major problems over spares and maintenance. A programme of rationalisation was put in hand to reduce the number of models, although these were still adapted civilian types. In 1934 the Einheits standardisation programme was instigated, to develop purpose-designed replacements for the various transport vehicles in service. There were to be a limited number of suppliers for each class of vehicle, and the vehicle was to be produced to a standard design regardless of the manufacturer – with the exception of the engine. This would always be that commercially available from the particular manufacturer; but the design of the vehicle should be such that the engines of other assigned makers could be fitted without major alterations.

In the case of the Kfz 1 standard light cross-country personnel carrier the selected suppliers were Hanomag, BMW and Stoewer. BMW of Eisenach built the original version, designated LE Pkw/325 (Leichter Einheits Personenkraftwagen 325, 'Light Standard Personnel Carrier 325'), which was produced from 1937 to 1940.

This was followed by the Hanomag model, the LE Pkw/20-B produced from 1937 to 1940. Meanwhile Stoewer of Stettin produced the R180 Spezial and the R200 Spezial. In 1940 all of the previous models were replaced in production by a new simplified version, the Stoewer Type 40. They were popularly known as Kubelsitzer, Kubelwagen or just Kubel – terms which later became synonymous with the Stoewer 40's successor, the VW Type 82.

There were four main variants in addition to the basic personnel carrier. The Kfz 2 was a radio car, the Kfz 2/40 a light repair vehicle, the Kfz 3 was a light surveying truck, and the Kfz 4 a light AA vehicle with three seats and twin machine guns on an anti-aircraft mount.

The Stoewer 40 was fitted with a Stoewer AW2 petrol engine producing 50bhp, and weighed 3,748lbs. Overall dimensions are: length, 12ft 7.5ins; width, 5ft 6.5ins; and height 6ft 3ins. The example illustrated on pages 21-24 is a Stoewer 40 Kfz 2 radio car with the original dark grey interior factory finish and the exterior overpainted in dark yellow according to June 1943 regulations; it bears the markings of Military Police Troop (Motorised) No.12 of the Luftwaffe's II Fallschirmjäger Korps. The camouflaged example on page 25 is a BMW-built Kfz 1 in the markings of a reconnaissance unit of the 2nd SS Panzer Division 'Das Reich'.

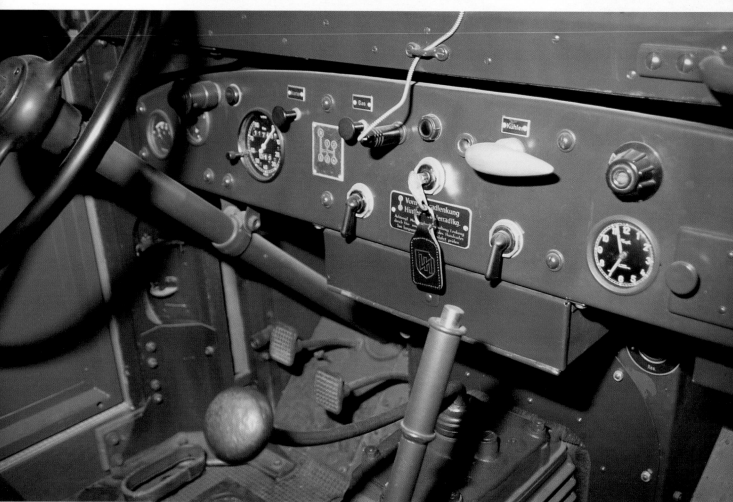

Volkswagen Type 82 Kubelwagen Kfz 1

The origins of the Kubelwagen lie with a design for a lightweight, affordable car created by Dr Ferdinand Porsche in the early 1930s. After largely unsuccessful collaborations with first Zundapp and then NSU, Porsche's design came to the attention of Adolf Hitler, who at this time was looking for a way to provide cheap cars for the German masses, for use on the new Autobahns. With the Führer's backing, the design progressed rapidly through the development process. Several prototypes were followed by the 30-strong Series 30 pre-production batch; and then by 44 examples of the Series 38 model, which were subjected to a total of over 1,500,000 miles of road testing. The production KdF-Wagen (Kraft durch Freude – 'strength through joy') was a small, streamlined, four-seater sedan, and after the war would become – under the more familiar name of the Beetle – the most extensively produced car ever manufactured.

The intention was to produce the KdF-Wagen at a rate of over a million units a year, and to this end a gigantic new production plant was constructed. Complete with its own power station and a new town for the workers, it was sited on the banks of the Mitteland Canal at the village of Fallersleben, part of the 14th century estate of Schloss Wolfsburg. The majority of the plant had been completed by early 1939 and production of the KdF had reached a total of just 210 vehicles when Germany went to war. Production of the civilian model continued on a limited basis throughout the war, reaching a total of 630 vehicles by VE-Day. The majority of the new Wolfsburg plant's wartime production was to take another form, however.

In 1939 Dr Porsche was asked to develop a militarised version of the KdF for use by the Wehrmacht. A new, simpler and more easily produced replacement for the Stoewer 40 light field car was needed as part of the Schell-Programm of transport rationalisation instigated in 1938 by General Schell, Director of Motorisation for the Wermacht. The job of developing the new vehicle

fell to Ferdinand Porsche's son, Ferry. The new Type 82 or Type 2 Kubelwagen used the running gear and floor pan of the Kdf with a modified suspension to increase ground clearance. Early production Kubels used the same 985cc, 22.5bhp engine as the KdF, but in March 1943 this was replaced (see below); top speed was about 50mph. The body was open-topped, constructed from ribbed flat panels by Ambi-Budd in Berlin. The design was ready for approval by December 1939, and prototypes were sent to Poland for field trials with the Panzer divisions. These proved to be a great success; production commenced in March 1940, a few examples entering service in time for the invasion of France and the Low Countries.

The Kubelwagen was popular in service, soon dispelling fears that its lack of four-wheel drive would make it a poor cross-country vehicle. Indeed, in the Western Desert it was generally held to perform better on sand than the four-wheel drive Jeep, and on the Eastern front its light weight enabled it to keep going over the heavy Russian mud when most other vehicles bogged down. The Kubel was used by all branches of the Wehrmacht, in roles including light reconnaissance, staff liaison, light transport, ambulance and assault engineer carrier, and production was to total over 50,000.

The Kubelwagen or Leichte Personenkraftwagen was fitted with a 985cc, 22.5bhp, 4-cylinder, air-cooled engine until March 1943; vehicles produced after that date were fitted with a 1131cc, 25bhp unit. Weight was 1,470lbs, and dimensions are: length, 12ft 3ins; width, 5ft 3ins; and height, 5ft 6ins with the folding roof raised. The darkly camouflaged example shown on page 27 and above bears the insignia of 1st SS Panzer Corps 'Leibstandarte Adolf Hitler'.

Volkswagen Type 166 Schwimmwagen Kfz 1/20

The Schwimmwagen was a development of the Type 82 Kubelwagen, and was initially intended for use on the Eastern Front where the poor roads and numerous waterways made a vehicle with amphibious capabilities particularly desirable. In the event the Schwimmwagen was also used extensively in the West. Mechanically the new vehicle was similar to the Kubelwagen, but it employed four-wheel drive instead of the earlier vehicle's two-wheel drive. The body was completely new: it was basically a watertight, welded steel tub that provided the necessary buoyancy. The vehicle was propelled in the water by a three-bladed propeller mounted on a stub shaft on a swing arm at the rear of the body, which was raised and lowered by a simple push rod. When the propeller was hinged down into position the stub shaft engaged a dog clutch on the camshaft of the rear-mounted engine. Steering in the water was achieved by turning the front wheels.

Early Type 128 Schwimmwagen were fitted with the 984cc engine; only 150 of these were built, by Porsche in 1940, for field trials. All subsequent models came fitted with the more powerful 1131cc, 25bhp engine, as the Heeres Waffenamt (Army Ordnance Department) had by this time set 25bhp as the basic minimum military requirement. The Type 138 followed, and eventu-

ally the Type 166; the latter was the major production version and, with a shortened wheelbase and reduced weight leading to an overall improvement in performance, it soon became the most sought-after model. The majority of Type 166s went to the Waffen-SS, since they were given preferential treatment in the allocation of equipment. By the end of the war 14,238 Schwimmwagens of all types had been constructed, the majority at Volkswagen's Wolfsburg plant but some by Porche's facility.

The Type 166 Schwimmwagen had a maximum speed of 6mph in water and 50mph on land. Its dimensions were: length, 12ft 7.75ins; width, 4ft 10.5ins; height, 5ft 3.5ins with the folding roof raised.

Kfz : K 2 s
Leergew.: 0·83 t
Nutzlast : 0·45 t
VL Kl.: II

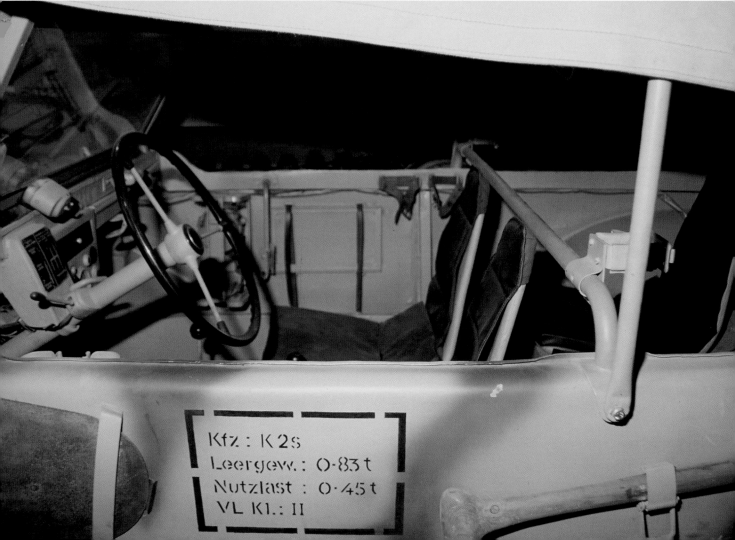

Kfz : K 2 s
Leergew.: 0·83 t
Nutzlast : 0·45 t
VL Kl.: II

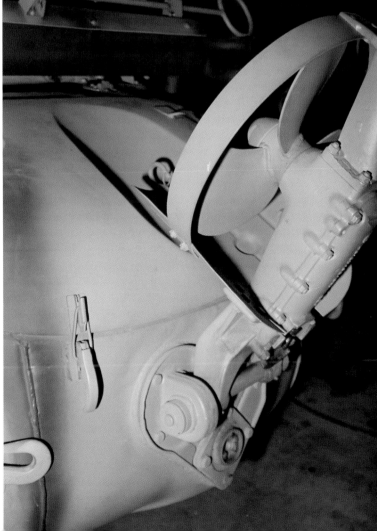

Mercedes 170V

The Mercedes 170 was the result of a commercial initiative to produce a small, affordable car more suited to the economically depressed markets of the 1930s. Designed by Hans Nibeland and his team of engineers at Stuttgart, this was the smallest engined Mercedes-Benz car so far – indeed, the smallest and cheapest built by Daimler or Benz since World War I. Moreover, it was to be equipped with all round independent suspension; the commercial need for a small car was obvious, but the adoption of an advanced suspension system was a brave move, and front and rear independent suspension in a series-production car would be a first for Mercedes.

The new 6-cylinder Type 170, announced in 1931, was the first of a whole new range of Mercedes-Benz models. It utilised a sophisticated transverse leaf spring independent front suspension, and independent rear suspension by means of a chassis-mounted differential, swinging half-axles and coil springs, though it still retained a box-section chassis frame. In its looks and performance the Type 170 was unremarkable, but in terms of handling and technical innovation it was a great advance. The new model also saw the introduction of hydraulic brakes, central chassis lubrication and

other details which would become common in Mercedes-Benz vehicles.

The Type 170 was soon joined by other derivatives such as the Type 200 of 1932, which was basically the same car but with a 2.0 litre 6-cylinder engine developing 40bhp. Nearly 14,000 Type 170s were built in five years, and the Type 200 was even more popular. A year later the Type 290 was introduced, and there followed numerous models of increasingly large engine size and greater sophistication. The culmination of Daimler-Benz series production passenger car design came in 1935 and 1936, when a new range of tubular chassis began to be introduced that owed much to the Type 130H series of rear engined cars. At the same time as the last of the rear-engined models – the 170H – was being shown, the more conventional front-engined 170V made its appearance.

Instead of the box-section frame of the earlier 170 and 200 models, the 170V had a tubular backbone frame, and a front-mounted 1.7 litre engine exactly like that used in the rear-engined 170H. The styling of the new car was restrained but unmistakably Daimler-Benz, and even though it was not at all forward-looking, production would be resumed after the war

and continued into the early 1950s. It was available with several different Sindelfingen-built separate bodies, including delivery vehicles and ambulances. Models built for military use included hard top and convertible touring bodies as staff cars and, under the Einheits-Programm, Kfz 1 Kubelsitzer field cars and Kfz 2 & 2/40 fitted out as signals and light repair vehicles respectively. More than 90,000 examples were built before production was suspended at the end of 1942.

The Mercedes 170V weighed 1.08 tons; it was powered by a 1.7 litre side valve 4-cylinder engine producing 38bhp and giving a maximum speed of 67mph. Overall dimensions are: length, 14ft; width, 5ft 2ins; height, 5ft 1.5ins. The example illustrated bears the markings of a staff car for the use of an officer of the Kriegsmarine.

Ford V3000S

As already mentioned, after the partial success of the 1934 Einheits programme a further rationalisation plan was instigated in 1938 by General Schell. Under the Schell-Programm it was proposed that procurement of all transport vehicles be cut back to a few models that were suitable for both military and commercial use. They were generally of simpler design than the sometimes overly sophisticated Einheits models they replaced, to reduce cost and increase speed of production.

The specification laid down for the standard medium truck called for a four-wheeled vehicle rated to carry 3 tons. It was to be produced in both two-wheel and four-wheel drive forms, the 4x2 being known as Type S and the 4x4 as Type A. The companies selected to produce the medium truck included Opel, Daimler-Benz, Magirus, Borgward and Ford Berlin, all of which produced both A and S Type vehicles except Ford, who only produced 4x2s. Most manufacturers gave their vehicle in this class the designation 3000 (the payload in kilogrammes), so the Ford model became the Ford V3000 S.

The Ford trucks were produced at various plants in occupied Europe and Germany including Antwerp, Amsterdam, Cologne and Poissy. They were essentially a 'Germanized' edition of the prewar American 1½-ton 4x2, rated at 3 metric tons for military use. They were manufactured from 1941 to 1945, with production being resumed for a short while after the war. Various austerity measures were introduced in the course of production: for example, many vehicles were fitted with flat section front mud guards, and in 1944 the 'Ersatz' cab known as the Wermacht-Einheitsfahrerhaus was introduced. This simple utility cab was constructed of pressed cardboard over a wooden framework in order to save increasingly scarce steel, and was designed so that it would fit all weight classes of Schell-Programm chassis. The standard 3-ton truck chassis could be fitted with any one of a variety of bodies; the official list runs to over a hundred types including GS, various house-type bodies, fuel tankers and aircraft maintenance vehicles.

The Ford V3000S/G198TS was fitted with 3.9 litre V8 petrol engine producing 95bhp. Its overall dimensions are: length, 20ft 1.5ins; width, 7ft 4.5ins; and height, 7ft 1.5ins.

The example illustrated here has post-1943 European camouflage and bears the markings of the 1st SS Panzer Corps 'Leibstandarte Adolf Hitler'. It is fitted with flat section austerity type front mudguards.

(Right) Another work-horse of the Wehrmacht in the 3-ton class was the Opel 3000 S, the famous Opel Blitz. Like the Ford it was fitted with a wide variety of specialist body types; this partly restored GS version is not yet fitted with its cargo body.

OM Autocarretta da Montagna Tipo 36M

The Italian army's first OM Autocarretta da Montagna, the Tipo 32, was introduced in 1932 as a 4x4 light multi-purpose truck, intended chiefly for use in mountainous regions. Produced by Ansaldo to a design by Ir.Cappa, the OM 32 was powered by an air-cooled diesel engine that proved very reliable and would stand up to hard service in extreme temperatures. It had independent suspension front and rear, and four-wheel steering. The gearbox was mounted amidships and drove the front and rear final drives directly. An example later captured by the British in North Africa was taken to the WVEE (Weapon & Vehicle Experimental Establishment) at Farnborough, England for thorough testing, and the cross-country performance was found to be extremely good.

The year 1936 saw the introduction of three new models. The Tipo 36P and Tipo 36DM were troop carriers; the 36P provided seating for ten plus the driver, and the 36DM seated seven plus the driver and was equipped with a pedestal-mounted AA machine gun. The Tipo 36M was similar to the Tipo 32 but was fitted with pneumatic tyres. In 1937 the Tipo 37, a slightly modified Tipo 32, was introduced.

The Tipo 36M was powered by a 1616cc diesel engine producing 21bhp. Its overall dimensions are: length, 12ft 5.5ins; width, 4ft 3ins; height, 7ft. This example bears the pre-war high visibility markings of the 'Edolo' Battalion, 5th Alpine Regiment, 2nd Alpine Division 'Tridentina', 110 Army Corps.

Steyr RSO/01 Raupenschlepper-Ost

The Raupenschlepper-Ost ('tracked tractor, East') was designed specifically to deal with the atrocious conditions on the Russian front. In the summer the roads were dusty, rutted, sun-baked tracks; in the autumn rain and spring thaw they were transformed into a morass of heavy mud, and in the winter they would be frozen hard and covered in several feet of snow.

The vehicle produced by Steyr was in effect a fully-tracked truck intended to perform the same roles as a conventional wheeled vehicle. It was fitted with a pressed steel truck cab and a drop-side cargo body, and the payload was 1.5 metric tons. For winter operations the vehicle was provided with wider 60cm snow tracks, but most photographs show the RSO fitted with the standard 34cm type. In 1944 the simplified RSO/03

model was introduced. Built and engined by Magirus, this had a flat panel open-top cab with a canvas hood. By the last year of the war RSOs were also being used in the West.

The RSO/01 was fitted with a Steyr 1500A petrol engine, producing 70bhp. Its weight was around 3.5 tons, and overall dimensions are: length,14ft 6ins; width, 6ft 6.5ins; and height, 8ft 3.5ins.

Typical of many gun carriages improvised in the later war years was the Panzerjäger RSO, a light tank destroyer. The Raupenschlepper's normal cab was replaced with a very low, armoured structure; and a 75mm PaK 40 anti-tank gun – minus its carriage – was mounted on the flat bed of the cargo body. The PzJg RSO, of which only 83 examples were produced, was mechanically identical to the standard vehicle.

Light guns

Three examples from the many types of ordnance towed by the field cars, trucks and half-tracks included in this book are illustrated here. On this spread we show the 3.7cm PaK 36 anti-tank gun and (opposite below) the 2cm FlaK 38 anti-aircraft gun; and on pages 54-56, the 15cm Nebelwerfer 41 rocket launcher.

The **3.7cm Panzerabwehrkanone 36** was the standard German anti-tank gun at the outbreak of war. Developed in 1933 and entering service in 1936, the PaK 36 first saw action in the Spanish Civil War. It was also sold in significant numbers to the Soviet Union until 1940, when exports ceased. The 3.7cm was a sound design that was widely copied by other nations, and although not very powerful it was highly manoeuvrable and easy to conceal. While the PaK 36 was adequate during the early war years, by 1941 more heavily armoured tanks such as the British Matilda and the Russian T-34 and KV-1 were proving completely impervious to the weapon, even at point blank range. There are accounts of Russian tanks destroying PaK 36 batteries by the simple expedient of driving right over them – scenes which no doubt gave rise to the German soldier's derisive nickname for the gun: 'the door knocker'.

More than 2,000 PaK 36s were in service by mid 1941, and a way was sought to prolong their useful life. The solution was the 3.7cm Stielgranate 41 (also known as the 3.7cm Austeck Geschoss). This was a hollow charge projectile and, since a 3.7cm hollow charge would have been useless, an over-calibre head was developed, carried on a long finned tail boom. Inside the tail was a solid rod that fitted inside the muzzle of the gun, allowing the tail unit to pass down the outer surface of the barrel. The propelling charge was loaded in a separate cartridge via the breech. The new round displayed an impressive performance, being able to penetrate over 7ins of armour. The only drawback was that its relatively low velocity restricted the effective combat range of the round to 300 yards.

The PaK 36 was a successful weapon in the early war years, and when superseded as a front line anti-tank weapon many were fitted to armoured half-tracks to provide fire support for the armoured infantry. In addition to the Stielgranate 41 the PaK 36 was also provided with AP, HE, and a tungsten-cored round, the PaK Pzgr 40. It weighed 953lbs in action.

The **2cm FlaK 38** anti-aircraft gun was a redesign of the earlier FlaK 30 produced by Rheinmetall-Borsig that had entered service with the German Navy in 1934 and the Luftwaffe in 1935. Experience in the Spanish Civil War and the Polish campaign had shown that the FlaK 30 would be much more effective if its rate of fire could be increased. Further development was undertaken by Mauser-Werke, since Rheinmetall were fully employed on other weapons. The redesign involved

little change, and was mostly related to the bolt mechanism; outwardly the gun appeared identical to the earlier model, and used the same three-footed turntable carriage. This was transported on the highly mobile Sonderanhanger 51 trailer, which could be towed by almost any vehicle. The gun was usually fired from the ground but could be fired from the trailer in an emergency. By the end of the war over 17,500 2cm AA guns had been produced.

Development of the **Nebelwerfer 41** began with the decision of the Army Weapons Office in 1929-30 to promote the development of rocket-powered weapons for military use. This decision put Germany several years ahead of any other nation in the development of rocketry, and the work of men such as Walter Dornberger and Werner von Braun was to continue to advance rocket science long after the war. The first practical military applications were for smoke screen projectors and grenade launchers. In 1931 the first spin-stabilised rocket projectiles were perfected, and by 1937 this led to the first examples of the multi-barrelled Nebelwerfer (literally, 'fog thrower'). The 15cm NbWf 41 was soon joined by the 21cm NbWf 42 and the 30cm NbWf 42. Latterly the 15cm and the 30cm were often mounted on vehicles, the 15cm either on the armoured Maultier or Schwerer Wermacht Schlepper, the 30cm on the Sdkfz 251 armoured half-track.

The Nebelwerfer offered several advantages over conventional artillery. As there was no recoil force to be absorbed the launcher and carriage could be of much lighter construction, which in turn made the weapon more mobile. It was simple to build and operate, and since it had no recoil stress it was very long lasting. Wartime rocket launchers were typically between one-

third and one-twentieth the cost of equivalent calibre artillery pieces. The missile itself was subjected to less strain, since its velocity was increased much more gradually than when a shell was fired from a gun. This meant it could have a much thinner case and so a much higher percentage of the total weight was explosive – anything from double to nine times the proportion of a conventional shell. Multiple launchers with rapid salvo firing enabled a very large amount of explosive to be delivered on target in a short period of time.

The disadvantages were that the rocket launcher was an 'area weapon', not accurate enough for pinpoint attacks; that it lacked the penetrative ability to deal with hard targets such as fortifications; and that its very visible back-blast of flame and dust and the smoke trails of its rockets made it impossible to fire from concealment, so that it had to be moved immediately after firing if there was any chance of counter battery fire. Despite this the 'Moaning Minnie' was extremely effective when used en masse to blanket an area either in defence or attack.

Over the course of the war the number of rocket launcher troops increased from 2,044 men in 1939 to 112,321 in 1945. The 15cm NbWf was produced throughout the war – a total of 5,283 in all.

FAMO F3 SdKfz 9

The largest of the German wartime half-tracks, the SdKfz 9 (FAMO F3 model) or Schwerer Zugkraftwagen 18t was introduced in 1939. It was the third in a series of 18-ton vehicles developed by FAMO (Fahrzeug und Motorenbau GmbH of Breslau), the first two being the FMgr1 and F2 of 1936 and 1938 respectively. Succeeding the F2 in 1939, the F3 was in most respects similar apart from its more powerful Maybach HL 108 TUKRM V12 engine, which produced 250bhp (this was also the engine fitted in the PzKpfw IV tank). The SdKfz 9 was used primarily as a vehicle to recover tanks and to tow the 24-ton trailers on which damaged tanks were transported to base workshops.

As the war progressed the FAMO was no longer powerful enough to tow heavier tanks then entering service, such as the Panther and Tiger; but it was retained in the recovery role for the Panzer IV and various assault guns. Until the introduction of the Bergepanther armoured recovery vehicle the half-tracks

were used in multiples, linked in tandem, for the recovery of Tigers and Panthers. At about this time some vehicles were fitted with a large earth spade to assist in winching out heavy tanks.

In addition to the basic recovery vehicle several other versions of the 18-ton half-track were produced. A few were used as bridging vehicles, carrying a crew of 15 and towing a trailer for bridging gear. There was also an artillery tractor version fitted with the typical open bodywork with bench seats and rear-mounted ammunition lockers. The artillery tractor was developed in 1938 when the first 24cm Kanone 3 appeared in service. These heavy guns weighed 83 tons in travelling order and were broken down into five towed sections, each weighing between 15 and 17 tons. The FAMO was also used to tow similar heavy artillery pieces as they came into service, including the Skoda 24cm Haubitze 39 and the Krupp 21cm Kanone 38. In Luftwaffe service the 18-ton half-track was used to tow the heavy 12.8cm FlaK 40.

The Sdkfz 9/1 and 9/2 were mobile crane vehicles. The 9/1 mounted a revolving 6-ton crane on a flatbed platform and was used by forward repair shops, recovery and bridging units. The 9/2 mounted a 10-ton crane and was provided with a reinforced chassis to carry the extra weight. The crane was equipped with a petrol/electric drive and a large counterweight, and the vehicle was fitted with stabilisers to permit the lifting of a heavy load at a reasonable radius.

The only armed 18-ton half-track to see service was the 8.8cm FlaK 37 (Sf) auf Zugkraftwagen 18t. This was an attempt to provide mobility for the 8.8cm FlaK and mounted the gun on a flatbed platform with fold-down sides. The sheer size of the vehicle facilitated all round traverse, and outrigger stabilisers were fitted to steady the vehicle when firing. Protection was afforded by 14.5mm armoured superstructure covering the crew compartment and engine. In all only 14 of these vehicles were built.

The standard FAMO F3 carried a crew of 9, weighed 18 tons and had a maximum speed of 31mph. Overall dimensions are: length, 27ft 1in; width, 8ft 6ins; height, 9ft 1in. The magnificently restored example shown here has standard recovery-type bodywork.

3

30 Km

Marschgewicht - 1513

Nutzlast - 2870kg

Anhänge - Gesamtlast - 1800

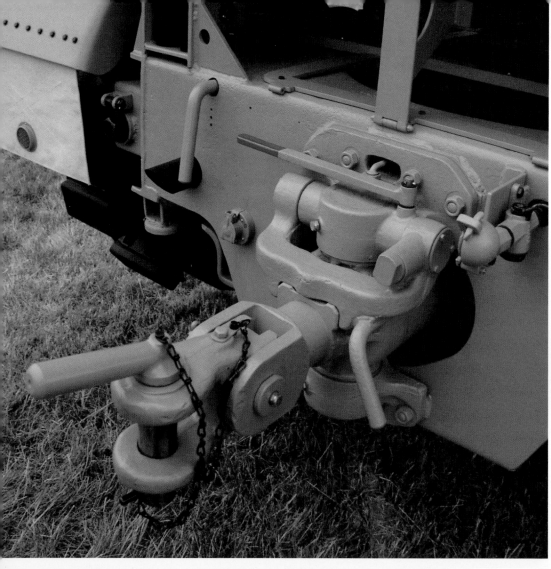

The rear tow attachment (left); and three views of the winch mechanism beneath the rear body, seen from behind (below) and from left to right (opposite).

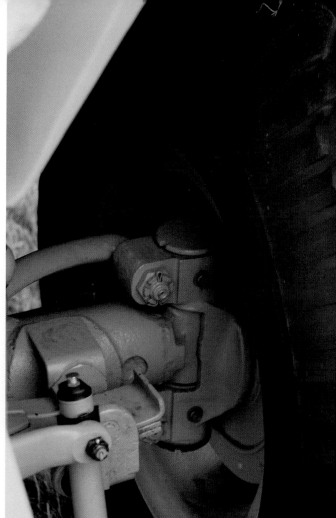

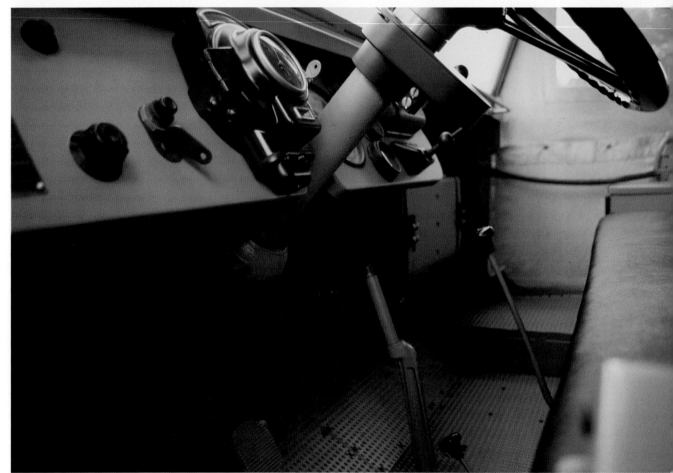

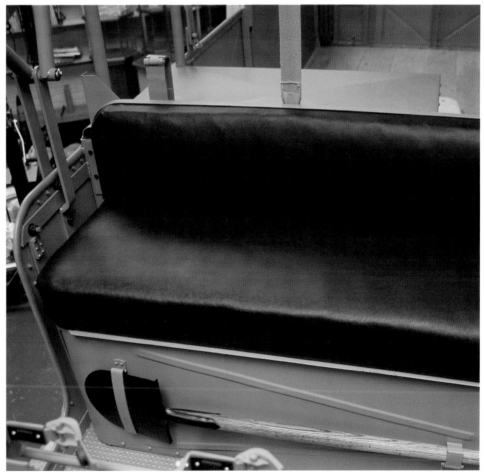

Demag D7 SdKfz 10

The origins of the Demag D7 can be traced back to 1932 when an Army Directive was issued calling for the development of a light semi-track artillery tractor capable of towing a 1-ton load. The development work was undertaken by Demag of Wetter-Ruhr, and the first vehicle of the series, the DII 1, was completed early in 1934. Successive developments over the following years led to the pre-production model, the D6, in 1937. The following year the design was finalised and the first production model, the D7, entered service. It would remain in production, virtually unchanged, until 1944.

The SdKfz 10's good cross-country performance and 1.5-ton payload led to it being adopted for a number of specialised roles, including a gas detector vehicle and decontamination unit. The Demag was also used as a self propelled mount for both light anti-aircraft guns and anti-tank guns. The light AA vehicle, SdKfz 10/4, mounted a 2cm FlaK 30 on a flatbed body with steel mesh fold-down sides. The later model, SdKfz 10/5, mounted the 2cm FlaK 38, which offered an increase in the rate of fire from 120 to 220 rounds a minute. From 1941 onwards the light AA vehicles were often fitted with an armoured cab and the gun itself was generally fitted with a shield. Since ammunition stowage on the vehicle was limited, a single-axle ammunition trailer was sometimes provided to carry additional rounds.

The anti-tank vehicles were not standardised variants but field conversions. Initially 3.7cm PaK 35/36 guns were mounted on half-tracks to improve their mobility, some conversions simply involved anchoring the entire gun, complete with carriage, to the rear flatbed of the vehicle. Other, more sophisticated conversions saw the gun removed from the carriage and mounted on a pedestal welded to the floor. As increasingly heavily armoured opponents eventually rendered the PaK 35/36 ineffective, some vehicles had their guns replaced with the more powerful 5cm PaK 38. Varying degrees of armour protection were provided for these vehicles, ranging from a simple gunshield to a fully armoured cab and bonnet.

The main role of the standard SdKfz 10 was that of light artillery tractor. The artillery pieces commonly towed by the Demag included the 3.7cm PaK 35/36, 5cm PaK 38, 7.5cm leIG 18, 15cm SIG 33, 2cm FlaK 30 or 36, 7.5cm PaK 40, and 15cm and 21cm Nebelwerfer. The Demag D7 was very successful in service, especially on the Eastern front, where its good traction and light weight made it particularly effective in difficult terrain. In all over 17,000 examples of the D7 were produced, mainly by Cottbus Mechanische Werke and Saurer Werke. Demag were initially engaged in its manufacture, but most of their capacity came to be taken up by production of the chassis for the armoured SdKfz 250 half-tracks.

The Demag D7 was powered by a Maybach HL 38 or 42 TKRM 6-cylinder petrol engine, producing 100bhp and enabling a top speed of 40mph. It had a crew of eight, weighed 4.9 tons and had a towing capacity of 1 ton. Overall dimensions are: length, 15ft 7ins; width, 6ft; height, 5ft 4ins. One of the examples illustrated is painted in pre-1943 grey factory finish, with the 1941 insignia of 1st Panzer Division and white tactical markings; the mudguards are, typically, picked out in white for high visibility, and bear a reminder of the correct tyre pressure. The vehicle in 1943 camouflage carries the yellow runic insignia of 2nd SS Panzer Division 'Das Reich' and the tactical markings of the 5th Company of the divisional reconnaissance battalion (Aufklärungs Abteilung).

Demag D7 driver's controls; and (left) inside of rear compartment with hood raised, looking back from right front.

SdKfz 250 (alt)

The SdKfz 250 was born of a decision, in 1939, to build an armoured version of the Demag D7 SdKfz 10. An armoured prototype of the larger SdKfz 11 – the SdKfz 251 – had already been built and successfully tested, and it was felt that a smaller vehicle would be useful for some tasks. The first obstacle to the design of the new vehicle was that the chassis of the D7 was designed around a Maybach HL 42 engine that produced only 100bhp. While this was perfectly adequate for the unarmoured vehicle, it was felt that the weight of an armoured body would degrade the vehicle's performance to an unacceptable degree. To overcome this problem it was decided to shorten the rear suspension by one road wheel and to reduce the length of the chassis, thus permitting the fitting of a shorter, and therefore lighter, armoured body.

Bussing-NAG, who had produced the armoured hull for the SdKfz 251, were commissioned to design a body for the new vehicle, and this was fitted to a prototype chassis provided by Demag. The new half-track performed well in tests and was immediately ordered into production. The Demag offered a slightly inferior performance to the SdKfz 251 and, of course, was less capacious, but it was able to take on many of the functions previously undertaken by the SdKfz 251, thus freeing it up for tasks that required a larger vehicle.

The SdKfz 250 first saw action in 1940 in the invasion of France, and was soon being adapted for a multitude of special roles. In all, the armoured 1-ton half-track was produced in 14 officially recognised variants as well as numerous ad hoc field modifications.

The SdKfz 250 was powered by a Maybach HL 42 100bhp engine, providing a maximum speed of 37mph; it could carry a crew of six including the driver, had an unladen weight of 4.3 tons and a payload of 1 ton. Armour protection was 14.5mm on the front and 8mm on the sides and rear. Overall dimensions are: length, 15ft; width, 6ft 2.5ins; height, 6ft 3ins. The examples illustrated on pages 79-95 are both finished in post-June 1943 camouflage and the markings of the reconnaissance unit of the 2nd SS Panzer Division 'Das Reich'.

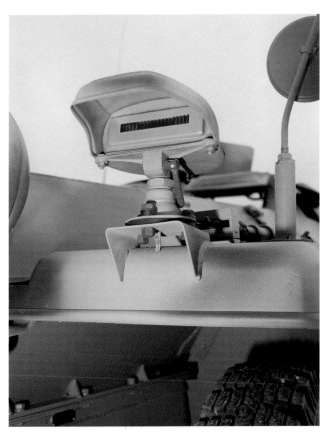

Die Kette ist so anzuspannen,
dass der obere Kettenstrang
auf den mittleren Laufrädern aufliegt,
jedoch das erste Laufrad
nicht berührt!

152 375

SdKfz 250 (neu)

I n 1943 a programme of rationalisation was put in hand to improve the efficiency of war production. To this end the design of many vehicles was to be simplified, and in the case of the SdKfz 250 this was to lead to a major redesign of the armoured body. The original production hull was of a complicated multi-faceted shape that was bowed out in the middle to increase interior space. The new design reduced the number of plates used in construction by almost half; the front and rear were now made of single plates, side stowage lockers were integral to the hull, the side vision flaps were replaced with slits, all mudguards were made of flat sheet steel, and the vehicle was provided with a single headlight. In this new form the SdKfz 250 was to remain in production until 1944, and remained in service until the end of the war in Europe.

On the introduction of the new, simplified vehicle the suffix *alt* for *alter Art* ('original model') was added to the designation of original production vehicles, and the redesigned half-track was known as the SdKfz 250 *neu* or *neuer Art*. The example illustrated is an SdKfz 250/5 radio vehicle.

2 atü

(Opposite) Simplified engine compartment plates – compare with page 80; details of exhaust, and lockers.

(Above) Simplified hull shape – compare with page 82; the protruding radio housing identifies the Sd Kfz 250/5 radio vehicle.

(Above) Looking forward along left side of rear compartment, from rear door (right).

(Opposite top) Looking backwards along right side, and (bottom) at inside of rear door.

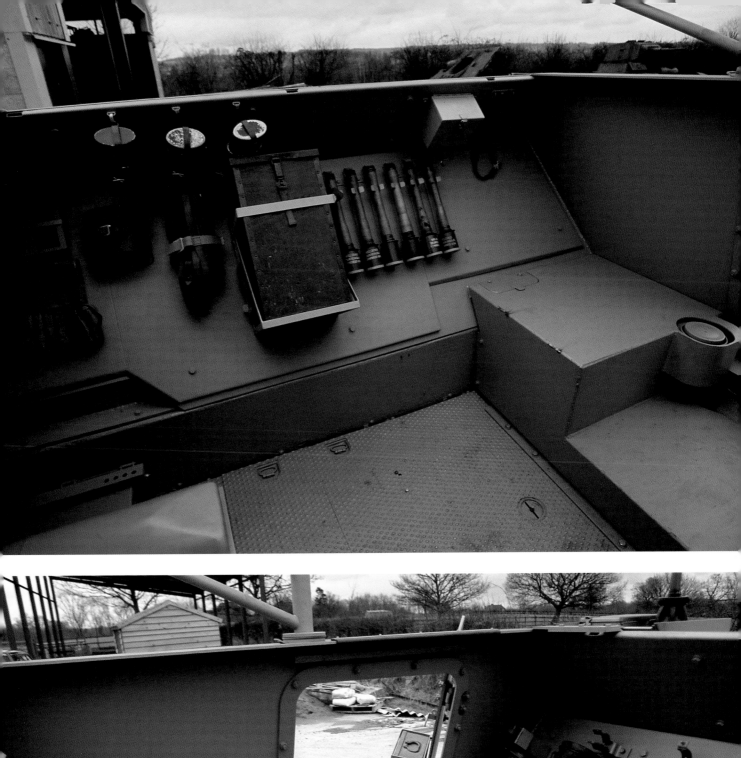

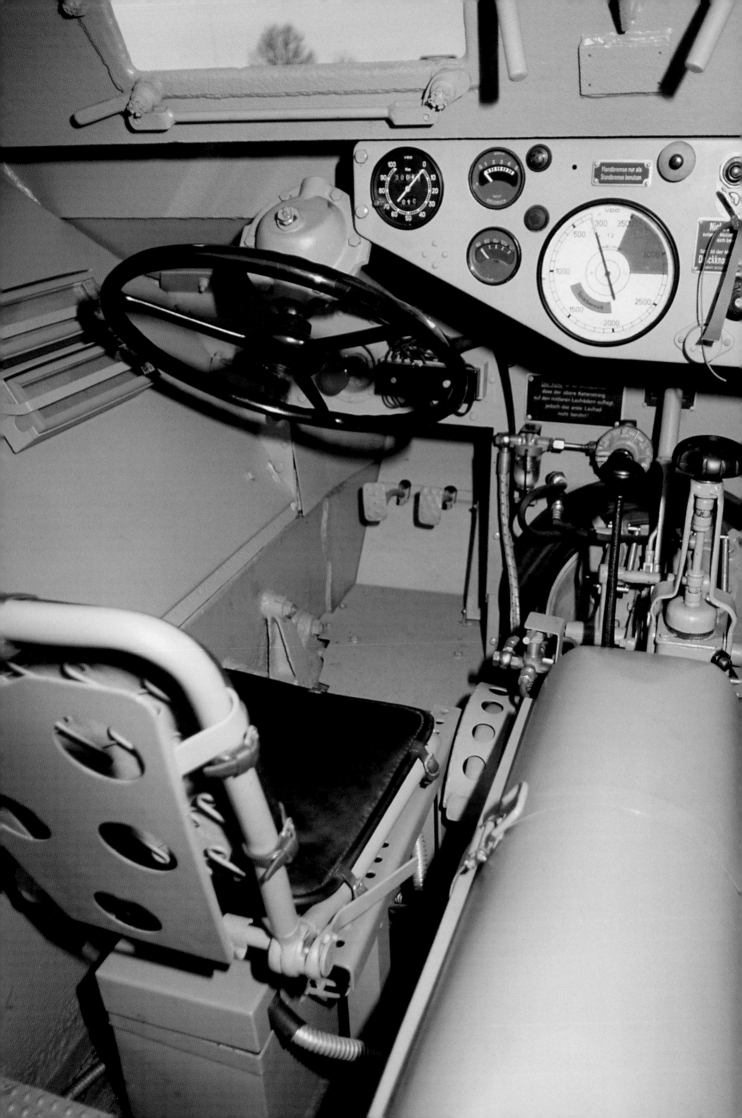

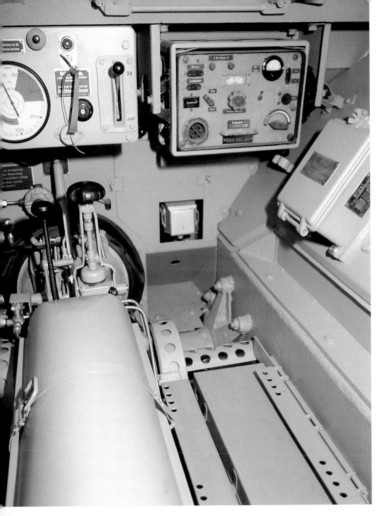

SdKfz 251 Ausf D

It was as early as 1935 that the idea first arose of developing armoured versions of the half-track artillery tractors then entering service, for use as personnel carriers. Of the six weight classes of vehicle available the first to be selected was the 3-ton chassis built by Hanomag (Hannoverische Maschinenbau AG), as this was the most suitably sized vehicle to transport a complete infantry section or squad of ten men. After exploring several alternative layouts, it was decided to use a front-engined chassis mounting a body with an open-topped rear compartment and rear doors. This would enable troops to disembark quickly over the sides or through the rear doors, and offered the additional benefit of using the 3-ton SdKfz 11 chassis virtually unchanged.

Work on the armoured personnel carrier began in 1937. Minor changes to the chassis were made, and an armoured body was produced by Bussing-NAG. This was of a faceted and well sloped design, heavily influenced by German armoured cars of the time, to maximise the effectiveness of the armour. The prototype

was ready in 1938 and, after successful trials, the vehicle was rushed into production. The first production vehicles entered service in the spring of 1939 and went to an infantry company in 1st Panzer Division for troop trials, which proved to be a great success.

The SdKfz 251 was to remain in production until the end of the war, over 16,000 being built by a consortium of companies including Skoda, Adler and Auto-Union. The basic vehicle was produced in four successive models, each incorporating improvements suggested by the operating experience obtained with the one before. The first production model, Ausführung A, is distinguished externally by the three prominent vision ports each side of the hull and the mounting of the aerial on the front right mudguard. It was fitted with swivel-type machine gun mounts at the front and rear of the fighting compartment, but neither was provided with a shield.

The Ausf B saw the deletion of two vision ports per side leaving only those for the driver and commander. The stowed tools and equipment were repositioned,

and a shield was added to the front machine gun mount. A bank of three external lockers was fitted each side between the track mudguards and the side of the hull, and the aerial was moved to a less vulnerable location on the top edge of the fighting compartment.

The Ausf C entered production in mid 1940 and introduced the one-piece nose plate and the prominent air intake bulges on either side of the engine compartment. In 1942 the Ausf D was introduced as the outcome of a programme to simplify the SdKfz 251/1 as much as possible in order to speed production and cut costs. The armoured body was redesigned to eliminate all unnecessary machining and fabrication time; faceted areas such as the rear body and the sides of the engine compartment were replaced with single plates, and the side stowage lockers were made an integral part of the body. The commander's and driver's side vision ports were deleted and replaced with simple slits backed by heavy glass blocks.

Operational experience soon showed that specialised variants of the half-track would be necessary to operate alongside the basic personnel carriers, supporting the activities of specialist units organic to the armoured infantry divisions. There would eventually be 22 officially recognised variants, and numerous field conversions and prototypes were also constructed. The SdKfz 251 was a highly successful vehicle, popular with its crews and effective in operation.

The SdKfz 251/1 was fitted with a Maybach HL 42 engine producing 100bhp, giving a maximum speed of 34mph. It weighed 17,182lbs; armour thickness was 14.5mm at the front and 8mm at the sides and rear. Overall dimensions are: length, 19ft 2.5ins; width, 6ft 10.5ins; height, 5ft 10ins. The vehicle illustrated is an SdKfz 251/1 Ausf D finished in post-1943 European camouflage, and bears the markings of a personnel carrier of the armoured reconnaissance battalion of 5th SS Panzer Division 'Wiking'.

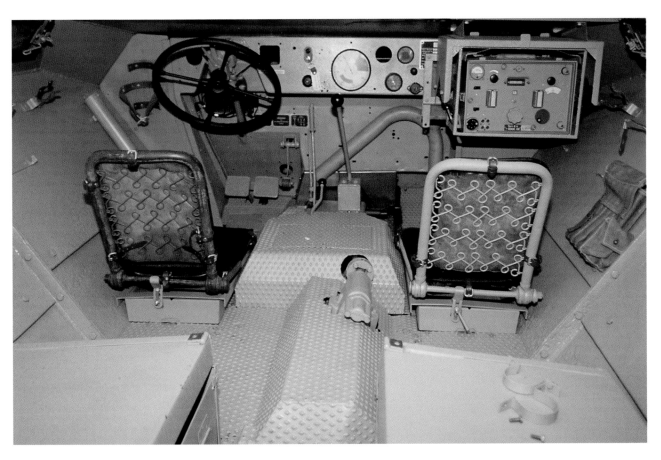

(Photographs by Roland Groom, © The Tank Museum, Bovington)

PzKpfw III Ausf L

The specification for a 15-ton tank, intended to be the mainstay of the new Panzer divisions, was first issued in 1935. It was to be armed with a 37mm anti-tank gun, but was to have a turret ring of sufficient diameter to permit up-gunning at a later stage. Competing prototypes were constructed by MAN, Krupp, Rheinmetall Borsig and Daimler Benz in 1936, of which Daimler Benz's design was selected. Ten production vehicles followed, designated 1/ZW Ausf A. These were fitted with a suspension arrangement consisting of five large coil-sprung road wheels on each side, which proved less than satisfactory. A great deal of development took place over the next three years before the definitive arrangement, of torsion bar suspension with six medium sized road wheels per side, was arrived at on the Ausf E. A limited run of 41 Ausf E were built, and after successful trials this design was standardised as the Panzerkampfwagen (PzKpfw) III.

By September 1939, 98 Panzer IIIs of models A-E were available and a few saw service in the invasion of Poland. Initial production was slow in spite of a manufacturing programme that incorporated not only Daimler Benz but also Alkett, Wegmann, Henschel, FAMO, MAN and MNH. By March 1940 there were 349 Panzer III gun tanks of all models (plus 39 command vehicles) available for the invasion of France, and the Ausf F had replaced the Ausf E on the production

lines. Little changed from the Ausf E, the Ausf F was the first major production model.

Experience in France showed the PzKpfw III to be seriously under-gunned, its 37mm weapon being ineffectual against all but the most poorly protected French and British tanks. Krupp had begun development of a 50mm gun for the PzKpfw III in 1939, and 40 Ausf Gs with the new 50mm KwK L/42 were rushed into action just before the end of the campaign in France – though too late to have much effect. Hitler ordered the further up-gunning of the PzKpfw III with the longer barrelled 50mm L/60 anti-tank gun, but new vehicles and Ausf Es and Fs returning for refit continued to be fitted with the short 50mm L/42 to avoid production delays. The end of 1940 saw the introduction of the Ausf H, which had the front hull armour increased by 30mm with the addition of appliqué plates. Wider tracks were fitted to offset the rise in ground pressure caused by the increased weight.

At the time of Operation 'Barbarossa', the invasion of Russia in June 1941, there were 1,440 PzIIIs in service of which 965 were initially employed. In addition to the standard vehicles some tanks modified for deep wading were used in the crossings of the River Bug and later the Dneiper. While the PzKpfw III could cope with the older Russian tanks which made up the bulk of Soviet armoured units in summer 1941, when it came up against the more powerfully armed and better pro-

tected T-34 and KV-1 it became apparent that the up-gunning could no longer be delayed. The development of the new 50mm L/60 tank gun was given added impetus by Hitler's discovery that his order had not been followed immediately. The new L/60 gun began to be fitted from November 1941, and the new PzKpfw III Ausf J also featured improved armour of 50mm thickness all round; this actually provided better protection than the 60mm appliqué armour of the earlier models.

The Ausf L was unchanged from the Ausf J except for the addition of 20mm spaced armour plates to the gun mantlet and driver's plate. A tropical version, with special filters and ventilation, was produced and was widely used in North Africa.

The next model, the Ausf M, was the result of redesign to simplify the vehicle and speed production; the side vision ports were omitted, as were the escape hatches in the hull sides.

By the end of 1942 the PzKpfw III was no longer viable as a battle tank; the final version, Ausf N – also known as the Sturmpanzer III – was built as a fire support vehicle. The Ausf N mounted the short barrelled 75mm L/24 taken from the PzKpfw IV, which had inferior armour-piercing performance to the 50mm L/60 but fired a more potent high explosive round. Some were also fitted with Schurzen spaced armour around the turret and on the sides of the vehicle.

The PzKpfw III formed the basis of several special purpose vehicles such as flame-throwers, command and artillery observation tanks, munitions carriers, armoured recovery vehicles, and carriers for engineer bridging components. It also provided the chassis for a number of self-propelled guns such as the 15cm SiG 33 auf Pz III, and the StuG III. Large numbers of captured PzKpfw IIIs were converted into SPGs by the Russians, who fitted their standard 76.2mm field gun in a squared armoured superstructure to produce the SU76i.

Production of the Panzer III gun tank ceased in August 1943, although the chassis continued in production for the StuG III assault gun until the end of the war; by that time some 15,350 chassis of all types had been built.

The PzKpfw III Ausf L was fitted with a Maybach HL 120TRM engine, producing 300bhp and a maximum speed of 25mph. Its armament consisted of one 50mm KwK 39 L/60 gun and two 7.92mm MG34 machine guns. It carried a crew of five, and weighed 20.8 tons; armour protection was 57mm on the turret front, 50mm on the hull nose, driver's plate and tail, 30mm at the rear and 20mm on the sides. Overall dimensions are: length, 21ft 6ins; width, 9ft 9ins; and height, 8ft 3ins. The example illustrated, captured in North Africa, now forms part of the collection of the Tank Museum, Bovington.

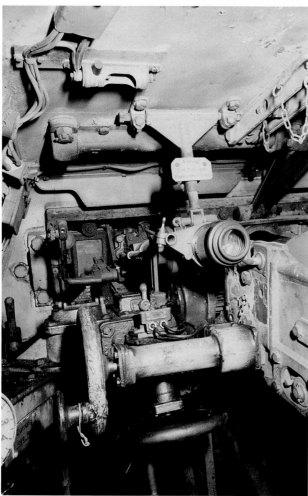

(Left) The gunner's position on the left of the turret, looking forward. The sighting telescope is mounted on the left of the gun; below it are the gun elevating and turret traversing controls; just visible at extreme bottom left is part of the 'clockface' indicator showing the degree of traverse.

(Opposite, top) Looking right from the gunner's position, showing the breechblock of the 50mm L/60 gun and the recoil guard – a lead weight at the rear of this corrected the gun's muzzle-heavy balance. The interior of this tank is structurally complete but is missing many smaller components and items usually stowed round the walls.

(Opposite, below) The gunner's seat and the foot pedal operating the electric firing control.

(Left) Looking backwards and upwards from the loader's position on the right of the gun, to the commander's cupola; note the heavy glass vision blocks, and the handles to operate their armour shields.

(Below, left) Looking from the gunner's position across to the right of the turret; note the roof extractor fan and the access doors. Low right is the commander's footrest/ seat, hooked onto the turret ring.

(Right and below) Looking from the loader's position on the right of the gun, across to the gunner's position and the left side access doors. Note the glass block which backs the vision slot in the forward door. Several spare blocks were carried, stowed in racks for quick replacement.

(Above) Looking from right to left into the driver's position in the left front hull. His KFF2 armoured binocular forward vision device is missing from its housing; a spare was carried in the box on the left wall below the left side vision block. The attachments to the left of this carried the driver's gasmask, and stowage bags for machine gun belts. The black housing between the side and front vision devices is an electric gyroscope indicating the direction of the tank.

(Right) The track steering levers each side of the seat; the bell shape left of the foot pedals is the final drive housing. The black-handled gear lever is to the right of the right steering lever, and above this is the intrument panel, facing inwards towards the driver. It incorporated a rev counter, speedometer, oil pressure and water temperature guages. Obviously, a seat cushion normally covered the springs.

Jagdpanzer 38(t) Hetzer

By the mid war years the strain on all German resources and the high rate of tank losses had persuaded the Wehrmacht to increase production of self-propelled guns – turretless tanks with limited-traverse guns mounted in a simple armoured superstructure – in proportion to that of turreted tanks. These SPGs could perform many of the tasks previously entrusted to tanks, from infantry close support in the attack to anti-tank combat in defence. They were quicker and cheaper to build, and their low, well-sloped armoured superstructure offered easy concealment in the 'ambush' situations typical of defensive warfare. The crews did not need such long training as those for turreted tanks, and were mostly drawn from the artillery rather than the Panzerwaffe.

The Hetzer (the name means roughly, 'Troublemaker') was the result of a specification of March 1943 for a light Jagdpanzer or 'hunting tank'. The production of the StuG III assault gun at Alkett in Berlin was severely disrupted by Allied bombing; spare production capacity was sought elsewhere, but although the Boemisch-Marische Machinenfabrik plant in occupied Czechoslovakia had spare capacity it did not have the

lifting gear or space necessary to build the 24-ton StuG. It was proposed that to maximise the use of the BMM facilities a new light Jagdpanzer should be designed that could be built there based on the chassis of the Czech PzKpfw 38(t) tank; this had been requisitioned by the Wehrmacht and had proved its reliability with several units in France and Russia, notably 6th Panzer Division. The design drawings were completed by December 1943, and a full scale wooden mock-up followed by late January 1944. At this time it was decided that the main weapon would be the 7.5cm L/48 PaK 39.

An order was placed for three production vehicles to be delivered by March 1944 – there were to be no prototypes, since the chassis and running gear had already been tested in the PzKpfw 38(t). The first three were delivered on schedule, followed by a further 20 in April and 50 in May. Despite some early teething troubles and the effects of Allied bombing, production rose rapidly, peaking at 434 in January 1945. The total produced by the end of the war was over 2,800 – a remarkable achievement in the circumstances.

In addition to the basic tank-destroyer there was a command version (Befehlswagen) fitted with an addi-

tional radio; and a recovery vehicle (Bergepanzer 38), which had an open-topped body with a large winch in the fighting compartment and, in later examples, a rear-mounted earth spade.

The Hetzer was a useful vehicle when employed in its intended role and operated by a well trained crew; but the cramped inside layout and poor visibility made the loader's and driver's tasks particularly difficult, and the very limited gun traverse (only 5 degrees left and 11 degrees right) was a handicap. Its compact silhouette made it easy to conceal and presented a small target. The thick frontal armour, powerful main weapon and good mobility were assets on the battlefield, but the thin side and rear armour rendered it vulnerable if it was used in unsuitable tactical situations. All in all, it had the typical drawbacks of a weapon that was not designed for its purpose but assembled from available components of other designs.

The Hetzer saw service both on the Eastern Front and in NW Europe, and 75 vehicles were also supplied to the Hungarian army.

The leichte Jagdpanzer 38(t) was fitted with a Praga EPA/ AC Model IV engine, producing 150bhp and a maximum speed of 26mph. It carried a crew of four, and weighed 15.7 tons; armour thickness was 60mm at the front, 20mm to the sides and rear, 8mm on the roof and rear deck, and 10mm on the belly. Armament consisted of a 7.5cm L/48 PaK 39 off-set to the right of the hull, and one remote-controlled, roof-mounted 7.92mm MG42 machine gun. Overall dimensions are: length, 20ft 7ins; width, 8ft8ins; height, 6ft 11ins.

The example illustrated here in plain dark yellow factory finish is a basic Hetzer tank-destroyer; it is marked on the glacis with the insignia of the Führer Grenadier Division. The camouflaged and more fully stowed vehicle on pages 113-117 is a Hetzer Befehlswagen, distinguished by the additional aerial on the left of the superstructure for the long range command radio set.

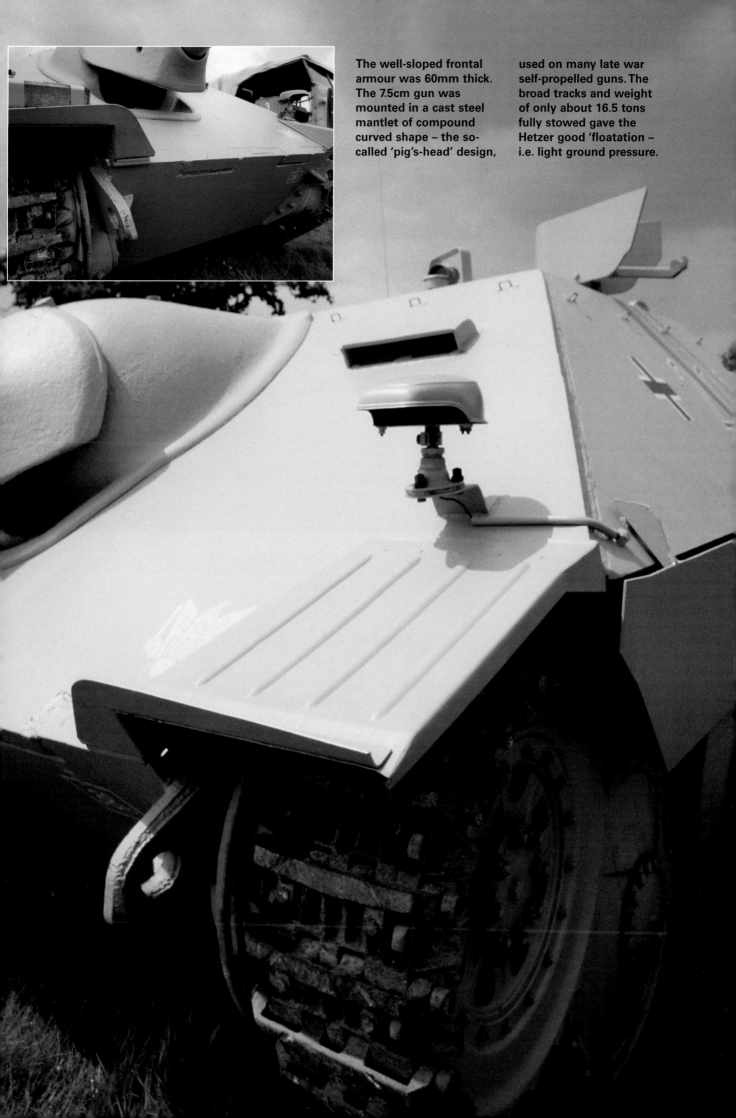

The well-sloped frontal armour was 60mm thick. The 7.5cm gun was mounted in a cast steel mantlet of compound curved shape – the so-called 'pig's-head' design, used on many late war self-propelled guns. The broad tracks and weight of only about 16.5 tons fully stowed gave the Hetzer good 'floatation – i.e. light ground pressure.

(Above and right) Although well sloped, the thin rear armour – not helped much by a few extra track plates stowed here and there – was vulnerable unless the Hetzer was pointed 'nose to the enemy' at all times. The limited traverse of the gun meant that the whole vehicle often had to be repositioned to keep targets in its sights. The small flap at top right of the rear superstructure was part of a small, split commander's hatch – too far back to give him good visibility.

(Opposite, below) Note the extra aerial for the command radio at rear left of this Befehlswagen version, with a prominent armour shield at the base.

The MG34 machine gun was remotely traversed and fired by handles inside the roof. The only access and escape for three of the four crew was the small split hatch immediately behind the gun – which could not be opened if the gun was not traversed sideways. The small size of the commander's split hatch is shown by the fact that the periscopic binoculars almost fill its front half.

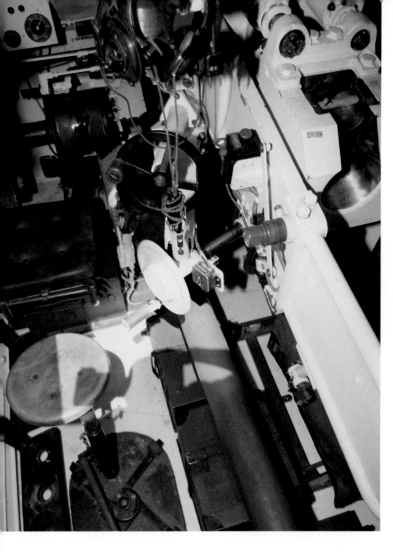

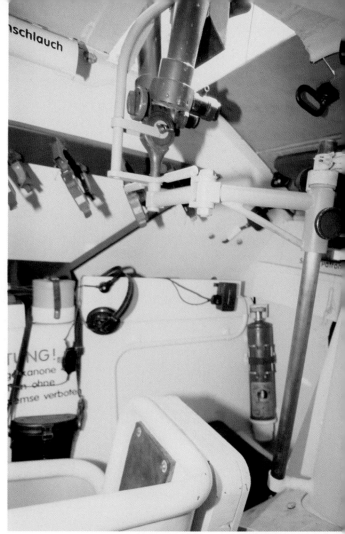

(Above) Looking forwards, on the left of the gun, where three of the crew sat in single file. The driver's seat is at top left, the gunner's stool in the middle beside his traverse and elevation control wheels, and the loader's stool just outside the picture at bottom left.

(Above, right) Looking from the loader's position back and right towards the commander's position, with his periscopic binoculars raised through his roof hatch. The gun breech controls and main ammunition stowage were both on the right of the gun, so the loader had to reach awkwardly across the recoil guard in order to reload.

(Right) Looking backwards from the gunner's position, towards the loader's stool, with the usual radio set on the rear wall, and right of it on the side the extra command set fitted to the Befehlswagen model.

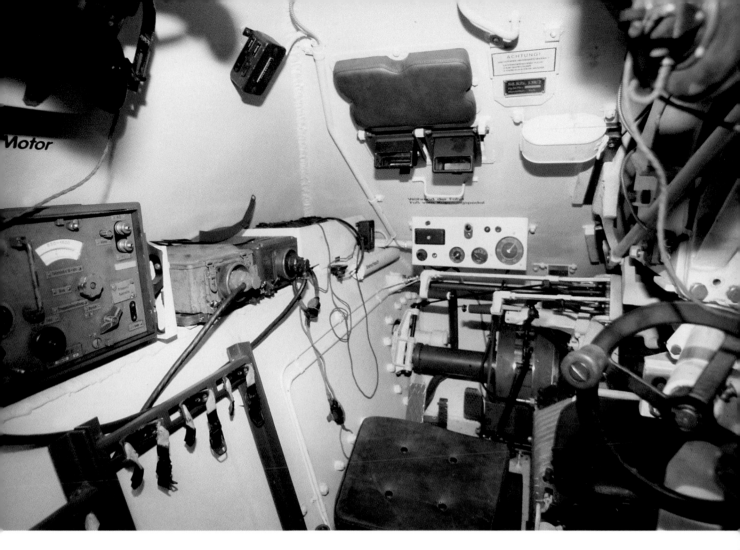

(Above) The driver's cramped position, with awkwardly close set pedals, and very poor vision from two small ports (below the pad). About the only good thing about the Hetzer from the driver's point of view was an advanced pre-select gearbox. In an emergency, with two other men between him and the hatch, the driver had little chance of evacuating safely.

(Right) Racked below the command radio are 50-round drum magazines for the MG34 roof gun. The small magazines meant that the gunner or loader had to open the hatch to reload dangerously often.

PzKpfw VI Tiger Ausf E

In 1938 development work began on a programme to provide a successor to the Panzerkampfwagen IV. Henschel & Sohn GmbH of Kassel produced the VK36.01, a prototype for a 36-ton medium tank; but initially there was little official support for the project, as the Heeres Waffenamt (Army Ordnance Department) was satisfied with the performance of the Panzer IV up to and during the Polish campaign. However, the invasion of France and subsequent encounters with Allied Matilda II and Char B tanks soon ended this complacency. Meanwhile development of a heavier, 45-ton tank had also commenced in 1937, but little serious work was done until a meeting with Hitler on 26 May 1941. Experience of British and French heavy types had suggested the need for a heavier tank; but after the invasion of Russia in June 1941 the Wermacht were soon to encounter enemies that made this a vital necessity. The Soviet T-34 totally outclassed existing German armour, and the development of the PzKpfw V Panther was a direct result. To deal with the slower, more massive KV-1 something even more potent was required.

In autumn 1940 a contract had been awarded to Porsche of Stuttgart to develop a 45-ton tank, with the pre-production series of six vehicles to be built by Nibelungenwerk. In February 1941 Dr Muller of Krupp secured an arrangement to produce the main gun and turret. The first prototype of the new tank, designated VK 45.01(P), was completed in April 1942; the second appeared in June and was sent to Kummersdorf for testing. The hull was of all new design; the tank

incorporated an innovative petrol-electric transmission, and the main armament was the 8.8cm KwK L/56, developed from the proven 8.8cm FlaK 18L/56.

In the meantime, on 28 May 1942, Henschel had received an order to produce a modified version of their VK36.01 capable of mounting the 8.8cm KwK L/56. This was to be done in such a short time scale that the only practical option was to modify the VK36.01 to carry the entire turret and gun assembly designed for the VK45.01. This forced Henschel to upgrade the design from the 36-ton class to 45 tons (subsequent design changes resulted in an eventual weight of 56 tons). This goal was achieved with surprisingly few changes to the original design, the only major ones being the fitting of the more powerful Maybach HL 210 engine, new fuel tanks and cooling system, increased armour thickness, and the sideways extension of the upper hull to accommodate the larger turret ring and radiators. The first prototype, designated VK45.01(H), was completed in April 1942, and between 26 and 31 October a body known as the Tiger Kommission met to decide whether the Porsche or Henschel vehicle should be selected for series production. After comparative trials Henschel's VK45.01 was chosen; and following an initial order for three pre-production vehicles, the first production Tiger was completed on 17 May 1942.

By this time an order for 100 Porsche-designed VK45.01(P)s had been completed by Nibelungenwerk, and of these 90 turrets were converted for fitting to Henschel hulls. Ninety of the hulls were converted to

(Photographs by Roland Groom, © The Tank Museum, Bovington)

Elefant/Ferdinand Panzerjäger; three were converted to Bergfahrzeuge recovery vehicles, three were fitted with Ramm-Tiger (demolition vehicle) superstructures, and four complete PzKpfw VI VK45.01(P) were retained for further trials.

The first Tigers to see action were committed on the Leningrad front in winter 1942/43; against the Western Allies it made its debut in Tunisia early in December 1942. Once initial teething troubles had been corrected the Tiger proved to be a robust and reasonably reliable vehicle. Its cross country mobility and ability to negotiate obstacles was equal to or better than most Allied and German vehicles of the period. Tactically it was to some extent limited by its voracious fuel consumption, and few bridges would support its weight. However, at the time of its introduction the Tiger reigned supreme in battle. Its gun far outranged any of its contemporaries, and its armour was virtually impervious to the weapons of all opposing tanks until the arrival of the up-gunned British Sherman 17-pdr Firefly and the Red Army's 85mm T-34 and JS-1. Not until the spring of 1944 and the appearance of the JS-2, with its 122mm main gun, was the Tiger outclassed, and by that date it was beginning to be replaced in service by the King Tiger.

From 1942 until 1944 Tiger units on the Eastern Front regularly achieved kill ratios in excess of 10 to 1, and were employed to devastating effect against Russian armour in defence of Germany. In the West the Tiger's fighting qualities were starkly illustrated by the famous engagement in July 1944 at Villers-Bocage. There a single Tiger of the 501st SS Heavy Tank Battalion, commanded by the tank ace Michael Wittmann, held up the entire British 7th Armoured Division, in the process destroying no fewer than 25 British armoured vehicles. The Tiger was ideally suited to the fighting retreat of the Wermacht that characterised the fighting in the latter half of 1944 and early 1945. Although the Tiger destroyed disproportionate resources from the opposing forces, it was costly and time-consuming to manufacture and was produced in relatively small numbers: the total completed was 1,355, as opposed to 6,494 PzKpfw III, 8,544 PzKpfw IV, almost 40,000 wartime T-34s and over 45,000 Shermans. However, its reputation was so fearsome that almost any German tank reported by an Allied soldier became a 'Tiger', and it had a psychological effect out of all proportion to its numbers.

The Tiger I Ausf E weighed 56 tons, and was powered by a Maybach HL 210 engine of 694bhp giving a maximum road speed of 23mph. It carried a crew of five; maximum armour thickness was 110mm on the gun mantlet and 100mm on the hull and turret front. Main armament was the 8.8cm KwK 36 L/56 gun, one co-axial 7.92mm MG34 machine gun and a second mounted in the hull front. Overall dimensions are: length 27ft 9ins; width, 12ft 3ins (on combat tracks); height, 10ft 4ins.

The example illustrated was captured in Tunisia in 1943 by 25th Army Tank Brigade and shipped to Britain for evaluation; magnificently restored, it now forms part of the collection at the Tank Museum, Bovington.

(Above) Looking to the rear of the engine deck with grills raised, revealing the Maybach HL 210 P45 21-litre V-12 engine and, at right, the left hand radiator and twin fans.

(Left) Looking into the engine compartment (rear at left, front at right), showing the large oil-bath air filters on top of the block.

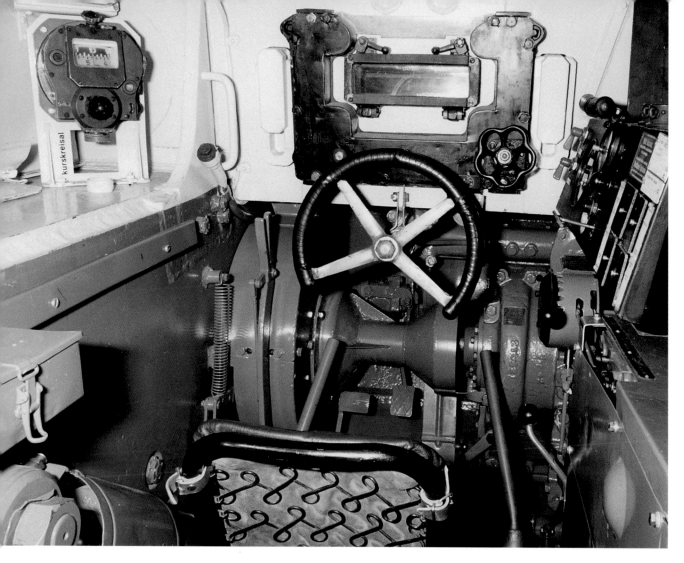

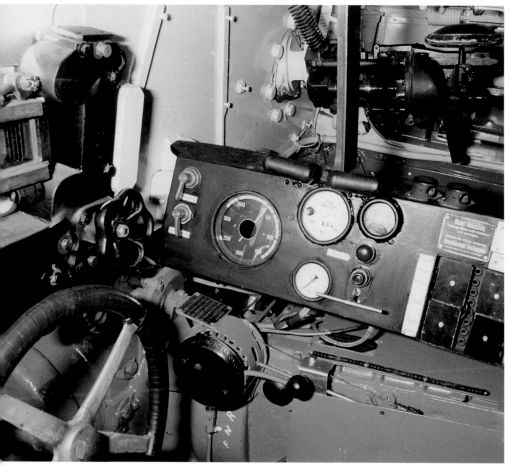

(Above) Driver's position, looking forwards. Top left, gyroscopic position indicator; centre, vision block above power steering wheel – the track steering levers below were for emergency use only. The black-knobbed lever beside the right track lever is the forward/reverse selector.

(Left) Instrument panel mounted on top of gearbox to the right of the driver's seat. The drum-shaped control below the rev counter is for the hydraulic pre-selector Maybach Olvar gearbox, giving eight forward and four reverse gears in each of three hydraulic cylinder settings. On the far side of the forward hull can be seen the machine gunner's position, with balance spring, binocular sight and head pad.

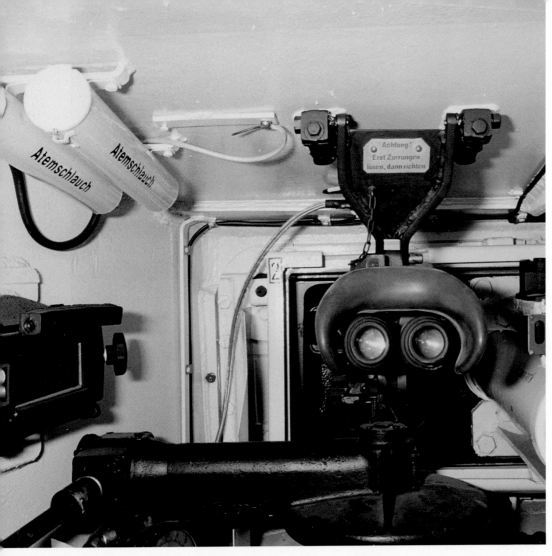

(Left) Gunner's position on left of gun, looking forward at the binocular sight, which had 2.5x magnification and a 23 degree field, and was calibrated up to 4,000 metres for the main gun. Just below it is the emergency hand traverse wheel; a foot-operated power traverse was normally used, but in an emergency the 20-ton turret could be cranked around by hand – it took 720 turns.

(Below) Looking from the gunner's position across the breech of the KwK 36 8.8cm L/56 gun, towards the loader's position on the right.

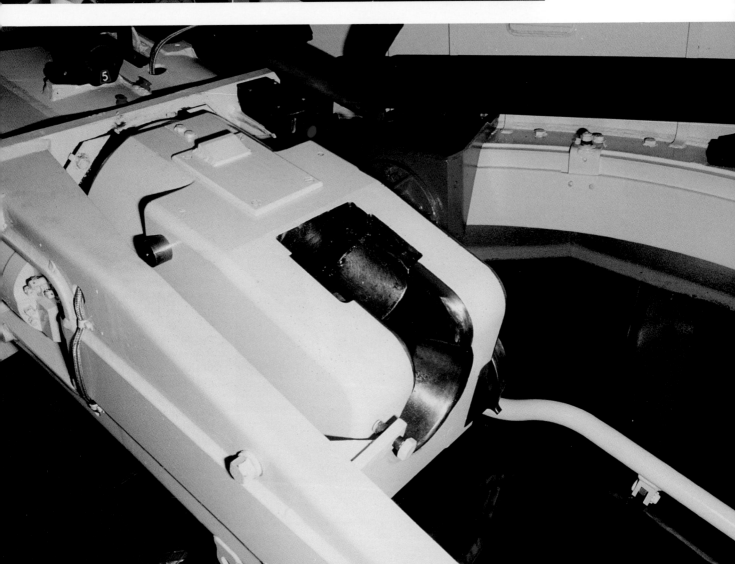

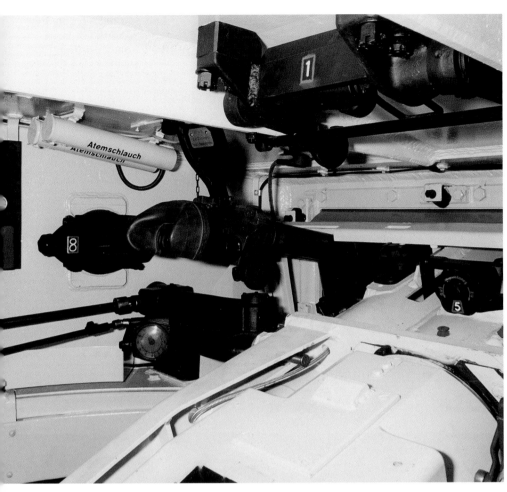

(Left) Looking left at the gunner's position from the loader's position. Top left plate with commander's and gunner's radio sockets and emergency battery for firing circuit. The horizontal rods link the gunner's to the commander's auxiliary traverse handwheel.

(Below) Looking beneath the gun breech from the loader's position, left across the turret floor towards the gunner's foot controls. At left is a water can (three were usually carried here); the central housing is the power traverse motor, linked by a rod to the foot control rocker plate; the pedal on the long curved arm is the co-axial MG trigger.

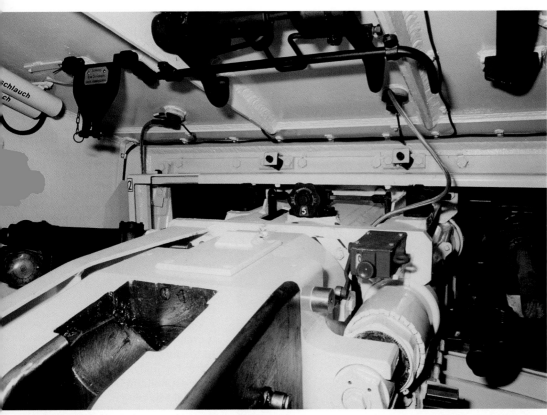

(Left and below) Looking forwards and left from the loader's position.

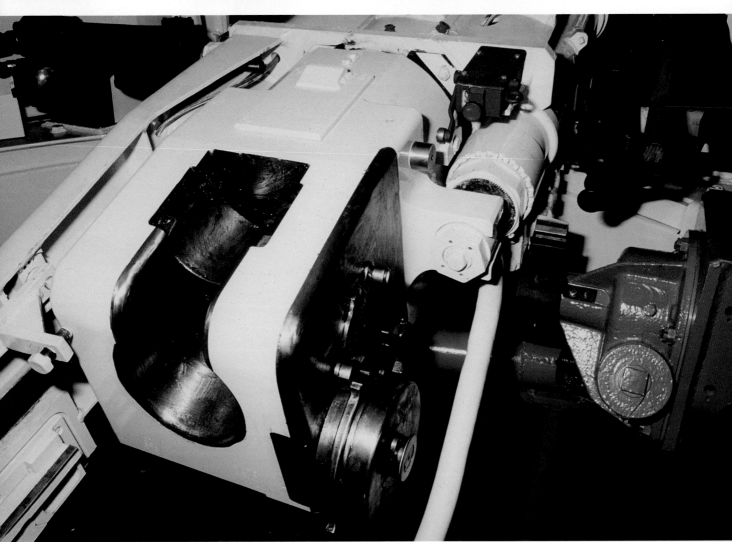

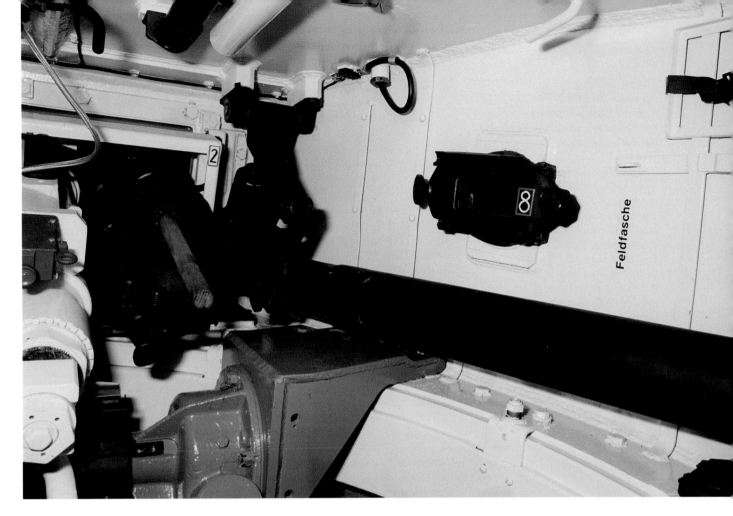

Feldfasche

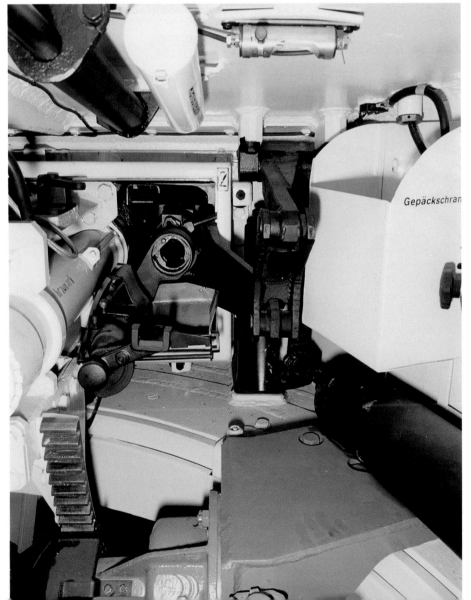

Gepäckschran

(Above and right)
Looking forwards from the loader's position – just outside the picture at the bottom is the backrest of his backwards-facing seat. The co-axial machine gun is missing here and a broom handle has been placed in its mounting in three of these photos. The grey-painted housing is for the right hand trunnion, connecting with the elevation rack. The black horizontal cylinder on the right holds the counterbalance spring for the muzzle-heavy 8.8cm gun.

(Right) Looking left and upwards, from the loader's position to the commander's position beneath the cupola.

(Below) The same angle, from higher looking down, showing the canvas tray fixed below the recoil guard to catch ejected shell cases. The stencil *'braun ark'* refers to the type of hydraulic fluid used in the recoil cylinders. The wire basket just visible beside the commander's seat is for signal flags.

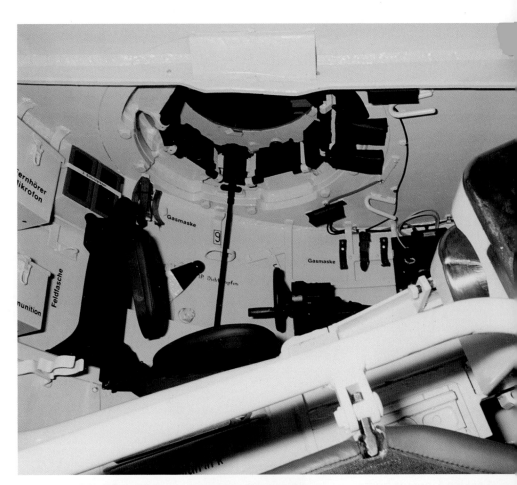

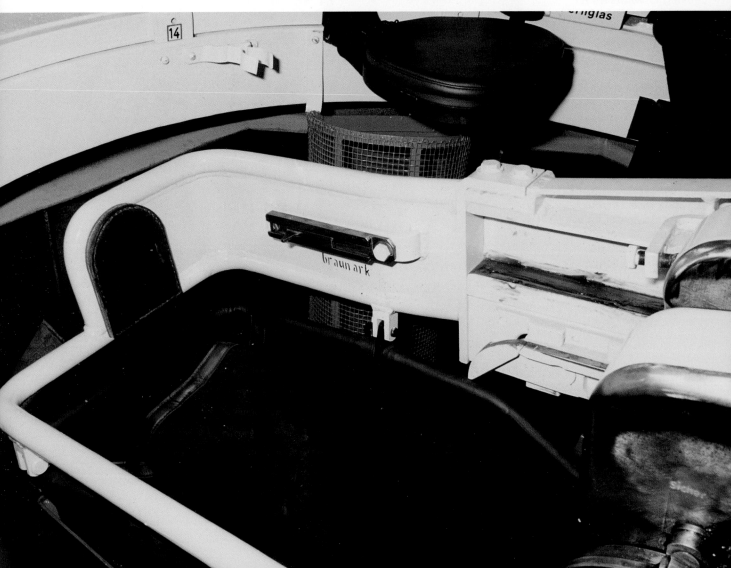

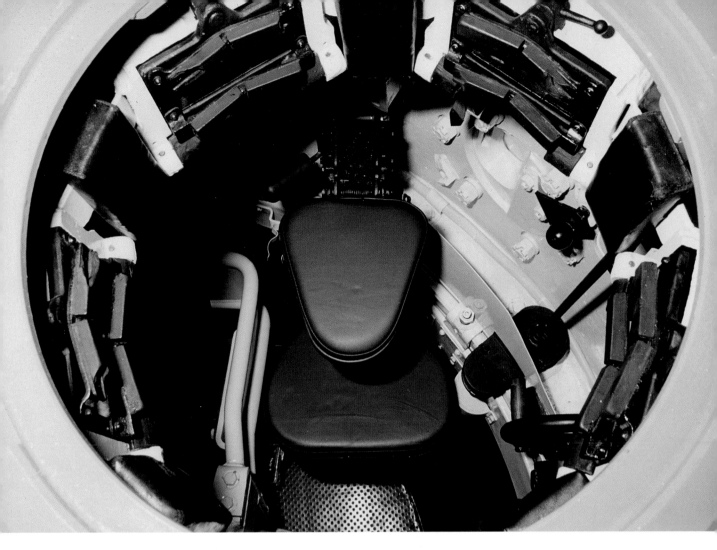

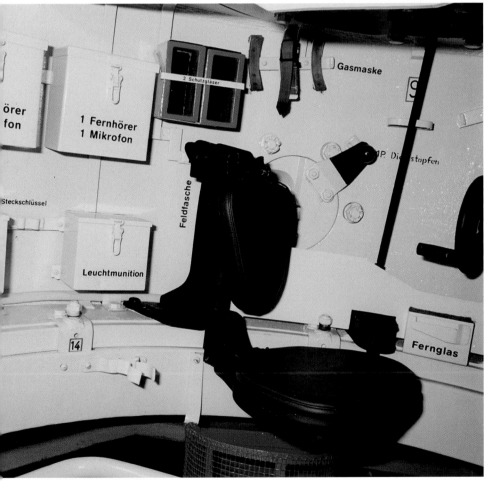

(Above) **Looking down and back through the opened hatch into the commander's cupola, fitted with episcopes all round. At centre is his flip-up seat, at left the gun breech guard.**

(Left) **Commander's seat and left rear turret wall, seen from the loader's position. The various stowage boxes and brackets are stencilled with their official contents:** *Fernhörer, Mikrofon* **(headphones and throat mikes),** *Leuchtmunition* **(flare cartridges),** *Feldflasche, Gasmaske & Fernglas* **(water bottle, gasmask & binoculars).**

Within image 2, visible stencilled labels: *Gasmaske*, *2 Schutzgläser*, *1 Fernhörer 1 Mikrofon*, *örer fon*, *Steckschlüssel*, *Leuchtmunition*, *Feldflasche*, *M.P. Durchstopfen*, *Fernglas*, *14*

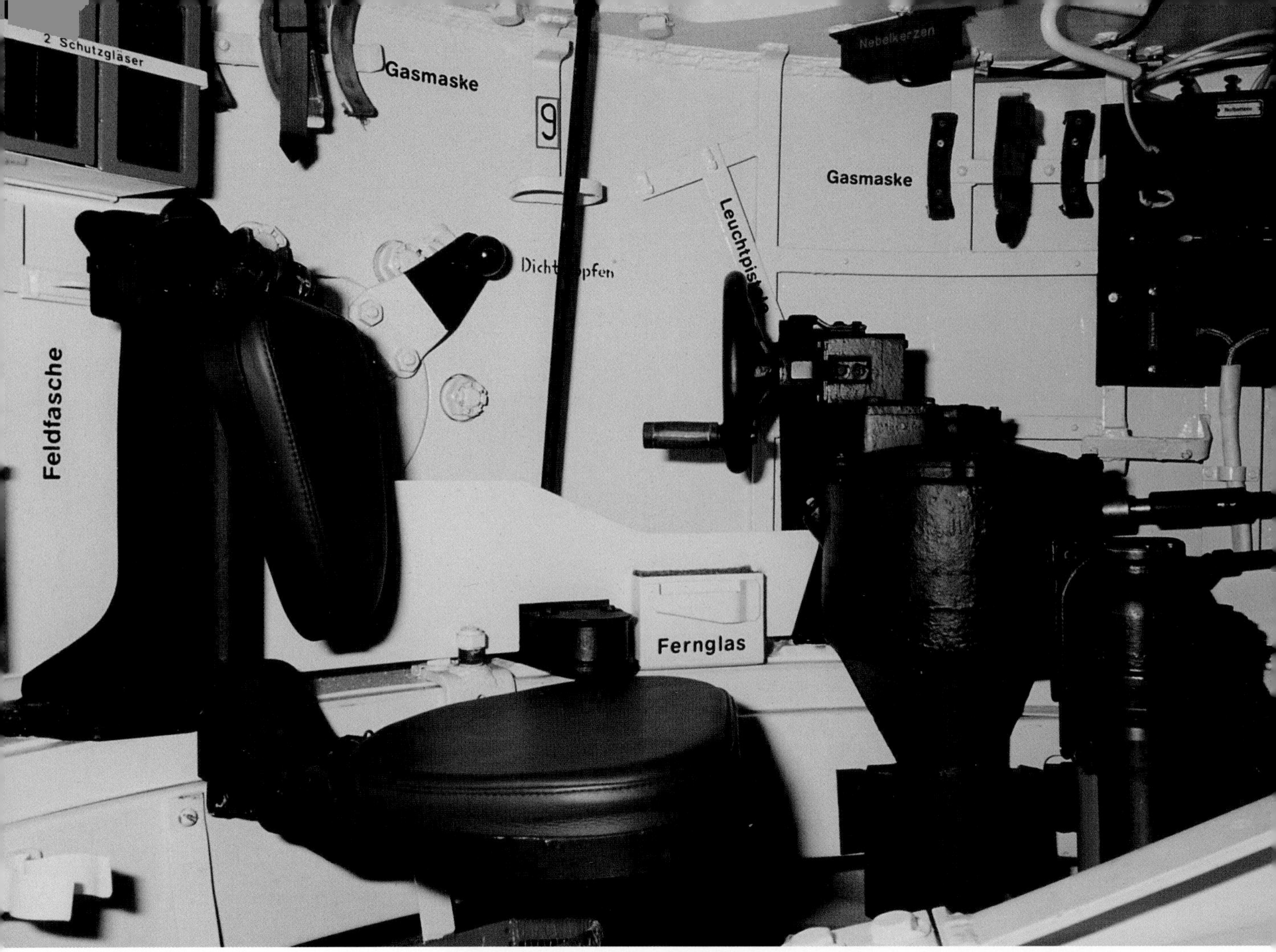
2 Schutzgläser
Gasmaske
Nebelkerzen
Gasmaske
Leuchtpist
Dicht pfen
Feldfasche
Fernglas

(Above) The commander's seat and auxiliary hand traverse control. The black vertical rod is the drive shaft for the commander's turret position indicator in the cupola.

(Right) Right rear of the turret wall. Left, hatch for discarding empty shell cases; extractor fan in roof; and turret main fuse box. Centre, stowage for MP40 sub-machine gun and a triple magazine pouch. To the right of this is one of the many stowage points for pairs of spare glass vision blocks – ***Schutzgläser***.

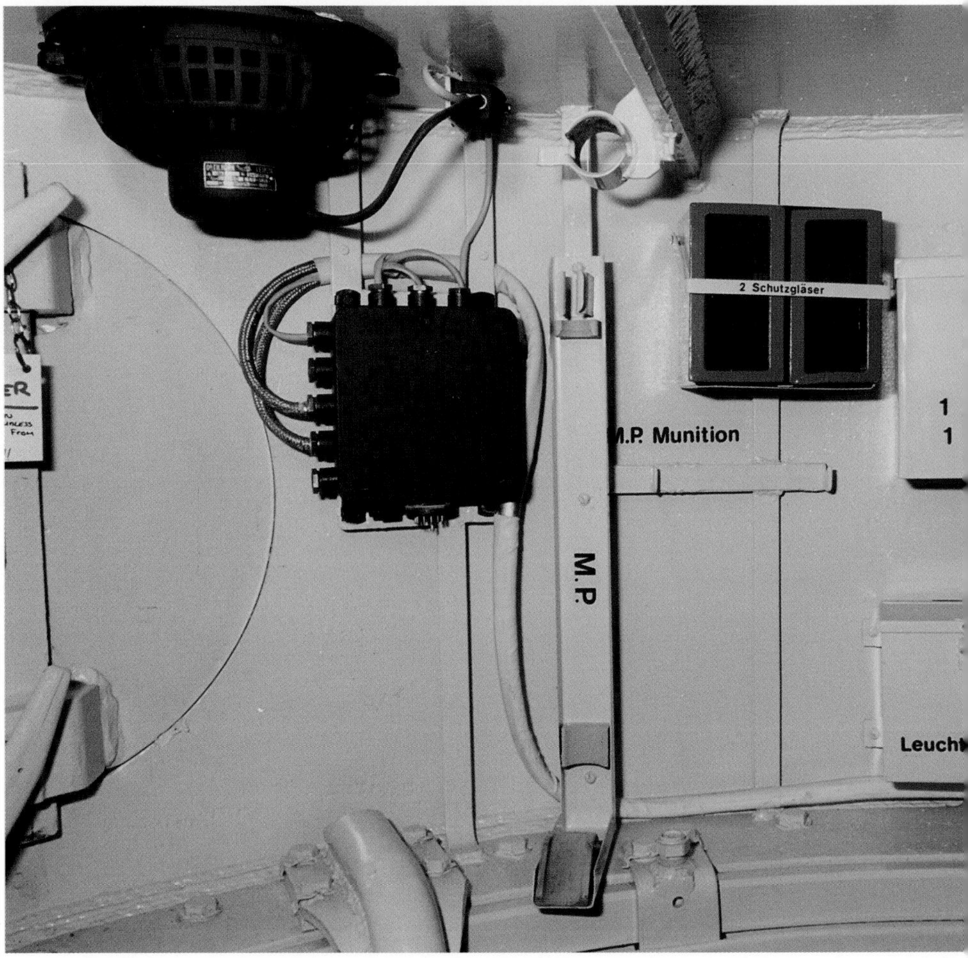
2 Schutzgläser
M.P Munition
M.P.
Leucht